Steck-Vaughn

BOOK 2

W9-BZC-893

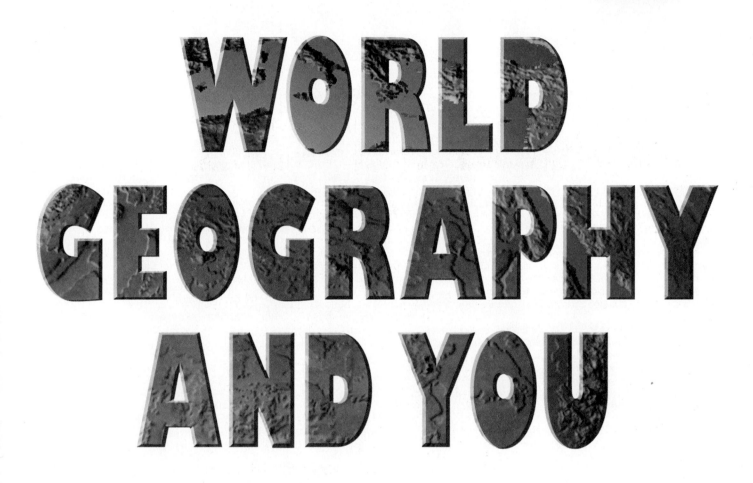

WORLD GEOGRAPHY AND YOU

Vivian Bernstein

Consultant

Jacquelyn Harrison, Ed. D.
Curriculum & Instruction Administrator for Social Studies
Round Rock Independent School District
Round Rock, Texas

STECK-VAUGHN
COMPANY
ELEMENTARY • SECONDARY • ADULT • LIBRARY

ABOUT THE AUTHOR

Vivian Bernstein is the author of *America's Story*, *World History and You*, *America's History: Land of Liberty*, *American Government*, and *Decisions for Health*. She received her Master of Arts degree from New York University. Bernstein is active with professional organizations in social studies, education, and reading. She gives presentations about content area reading to school faculties and professional groups. Bernstein was a teacher in the New York City Public School System for a number of years.

STAFF CREDITS

Executive Editor: Ellen Northcutt

Design Manager: Rusty Kaim

Photo Editor: Margie Foster

Electronic Production: Jill Klinger

ACKNOWLEDGEMENTS

Cartography: GeoSystems, Inc.

Flags: © The Flag Folio

Photography Credits: (KEY: C=Corbis; CL=Corel; SS=Superstock)

P. 1 (left) © Gregory G. Dimijian/Photo Researchers, (right) © David Madison/Bruce Coleman, Inc.; p. 3 © David Madison/Bruce Coleman; p. 4 (right) © SS, (left) © P. Ward/Bruce Coleman, Inc.; p. 5 (right) © J.C. Carton/Bruce Coleman, Inc., (left) © Nik Wheeler/C; p. 6 (top) © Michael Lichter/International Stock, (bottom) © David Turnley; Detroit Free Press/Black Star; p. 11 © CL; p. 12 (right) © Gilbert/Sygma, (left) © CL; p. 13 (both) © SS; p. 14 (top) © SS, (bottom) © Harvey Lloyd/The Stock Market; p. 19 © John Shaw/Bruce Coleman, Inc.; p. 20 (top) © The Purcell Team/C, (bottom) © Bill Ruth/Bruce Coleman, Inc.; p. 21 (top) © Daryl Balfour; ABPL/C, (bottom) © Kennan Ward Photography/C; p. 22 (top) © J.C. Carton/Bruce Coleman, Inc., (bottom) © John Shaw/Bruce Coleman, Inc.; p. 27 © Bucky Reeves; National Audubon Society/Photo Researchers; p. 28 (top) © Paul Almasy/C, (bottom) © SS; p. 29 (top) © SS, (bottom) © S. Peterson/Gamma Liaison; p. 30 (top) © Howard Davies/C, (bottom) © Photonews/Gamma Liaison; p. 34 © SS; p. 35 © David Barritt/Gamma Liaison; p. 36 (top) © Hans Georg Roth/C, (bottom) © Renault/Rieger/Gamma Liaison; p. 37 (top) © SS, (bottom) © Lisa Trocchi; ABPL/C; p. 42 (top) © Gamma Liaison, (bottom) © Chad Ehlers/International Stock; p. 43 (top) © M.J. Griffith/Photo Researchers, (bottom) © Anthony Bannister, ABPL/C; p. 44 (top) © Martin Dohrn/Photo Researchers, (bottom) © Wendy Stone/Gamma Liaison; p. 45 (both) © Liba Taylor/C; p. 46 © SS; p. 49 (top) © Charles & Josette Lenars/C, (bottom) © Steve Kaufman/C; p. 51 © Roberto Arakaki/International Stock; p. 52 (top) © Steve Kaufman/C, (bottom) © Ray Ellis/Photo Researchers; p. 53 (top) © C, (bottom) © Bojan Brecelj/C; p. 54 (top) © Robert Holmes/C, (bottom) © Bill Lyons/Photo Researchers; p. 58 © Gerhardt Liebmann/Photo Researchers; p. 59 (top) © World Perspectives/Explorer/Photo Researchers, (bottom) © E. R. Degginger/Bruce Coleman, Inc.; p. 60 (top) © Dave Bartruff/C, (bottom) © Hamilton Wright/Photo Researchers; p. 61 (top) © Joseph Horner/C, (bottom) © Chuck Szymanski/International Stock; p. 62 (top) © Richard Nowitz/C, (bottom) © Nik Wheeler/C; pp. 67, 68 (top) © Richard T. Nowitz/C; p. 68 (bottom) © Larousse/Photo Researchers; p. 69 (top) © Morton Beebe-S.F./C, (bottom) © Richard T. Nowitz/C; p. 70 (top) © Dave Bartruff/C, (bottom) © David Wells/C; p. 71 © Richard T. Nowitz/C; p. 76 © Sidali-Djenidi/Gamma Liaison; p. 77 (top) © CL, (bottom) © SS; p. 78 (top) © Adam Woolfitt/C, (bottom) © SS; p. 79 (top) © Bill Cardoni/Liaison International, (bottom) © Robert Nickelsberg/Gamma Liaison; p. 84 © Arthur Thevenart/C; p. 85 (top) © Gamma Liaison, (bottom) © Ray Ellis/Photo Researchers; p. 86 (top) © Gamma Liaison, (bottom) © Sygma-Paris; p. 87 (top) © Eric Bouvet/Gamma Liaison, (bottom) © Chip Hires/Gamma Liaison; p. 92 (top) © Richard T. Nowitz/C, (bottom) Nik Wheeler/C; p. 93 (top) © SS, (bottom) © Robin Adshead; The Military Picture Library/C; p. 94 (top) © Nik Wheeler/C, (bottom) © Massey/Spooner/Gamma Liaison; p. 97 (top) © SS, (bottom) © The Stock Market; pp. 99, 100 (top) © SS; p. 100 (bottom) © Roger Wood/C; p. 101 (top) © SS, (bottom) © Fletcher & Baylis/Photo Researchers; p. 102 (both) © SS; p. 106 © James P. Blair/National Geographic Image Collection; p. 107 (top) © CL, (bottom) © SS; p. 108 (top) © James P. Blair/National Geographic Image Collection, (bottom) © Hulton-Deutsch Collection/C; p. 109 (top) © Alvaro de Leiva/Liaison International, (bottom) © SS; p. 110 © Dennis Brack/Black Star; p. 115 © Joe Viesti/Viesti Associates, Inc.; p. 116 (top) © National Geographic Society, (bottom) © Charles Bonnay/Black Star; p. 117 (top) © Patrick Bar/Gamma Liaison, (bottom) © Frederick Ayer/Photo Researchers; p. 118 (top) © Joe Smoljan/International Stock, (bottom) © Dave Bartruff/C; p. 123 © SS; p. 124 (top) © Dan Lamont/C, (bottom) © Nancy Sefton/Photo Researchers; (top) © Bob Nickelsberg/Gamma Liaison, (bottom) © Christian Grizimek/OKAPIA/Photo Researchers; p. 126 (top) © Nik Wheeler/C, (bottom) © Andrea Brizzi/The Stock Market; p. 131 (top) © Porterfield/Chickering/Photo Researchers, (bottom) Earl & Nazima Kowall/C; p. 132 (top) © Joel W. Rogers/C, (bottom) © SS; p. 133 (top) © Kevin Morris/C, (bottom) © Nik Wheeler/C; pp. 137 (both), 139 © SS; p. 140 (top) © G. Brad Lewis/Liaison International, (bottom) © Michael Yamashita/West Light; p. 141 (top) © Michael Yamashita/C, (bottom) © USGS-Hawaii Volcano Observatory/C; p. 142 © Buck Kelly/Liaison International; p. 146 © Kevin Morris/C; pp. 147 (both), 148 (top) © SS; p. 148 (bottom) © Wolfgang Kaehler/C; p. 149 (top) © Erica Lansner/Black Star, (bottom) © Jack Fields/C; p. 150 (top) © Francois Perri/Gamma Liaison, (bottom) © AP Photo/Zinhua; p. 155 © SS; p. 156 (top) © Michael Yamashita/C, (bottom) © Paul Berry/C; p. 157 (top) © Morimoto/Gamma Liaison, (bottom) © Michael Yamashita/C; p. 158 (both) © SS; p. 164 © Brent Bear; p. 165 (top) © Anthony Suau/Gamma Liaison, (bottom) © Ron McMillan/Gamma Liaison; p. 166 (top) © SS, (bottom) © Anthony Suau/Gamma Liaison; p. 171 © A.P.L./Westlight; p. 172 (top) © Ralph A. Clevenger/Westlight, (bottom) © SS; p. 173 (top) © SS, (bottom) © David Burnett/The Stock Market; p. 174 (top) © Michael Coyne/Black Star, (bottom) © SS; p. 179 © Nik Wheeler/C; p. 180 (top) © Richard Pharaoh/International Stock Photo, (bottom) © Mark Greenberg/Liaison International; p. 181 (top) © Chris Rainier/C, (bottom) © Zefa Germany/The Stock Market; p. 185 (top) © Masha Nordbye/Bruce Coleman, Inc., (bottom) © Alison Wright/C; p. 186 (top) © Alison Wright/C, (bottom) © SS; p. 187 (top) © Michael Yamashita/C, (bottom) © Richard Holmes/C.

CONTENTS

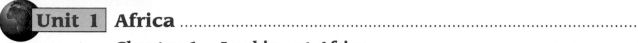

Special Places

Biography

Skill Builder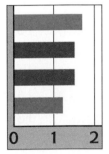

Maps

Charts, Graphs, and Diagrams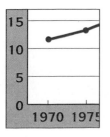

Africa

Victoria Falls

Mount Kilimanjaro

DID YOU KNOW?

▲ Africa has more countries than any other continent.

▲ The Sahara is a desert that is the size of the United States. It is the world's largest desert.

▲ Most of the world's gold and diamonds come from Africa.

▲ More than 800 languages are spoken in Africa.

▲ Victoria Falls drops about 350 feet. Africans call the falls *Mosi oa Toenja,* which means "smoke that thunders."

▲ The country of South Africa has three capital cities.

WRITE A TRAVELOGUE

Africa has many countries and many different cultures. It has many kinds of animals, plants, and minerals. Look at the photographs of Africa in this unit. Choose two places that you would like to visit. Write a paragraph in your travelogue that tells why those two places are interesting to you. After reading the unit, write two paragraphs in your travelogue that describe how life in Africa is affected by the climates and landforms found there.

THEME: HUMAN/ENVIRONMENTAL INTERACTION

Looking at Africa

Think About As You Read

1. What are Africa's landforms and rivers?
2. What kinds of climates and plant life are found in Africa?
3. How is North Africa different from the region south of the Sahara?

New Words

- ◆ vegetation
- ◆ savannas
- ◆ semiarid
- ◆ Sahel
- ◆ grasslands
- ◆ droughts
- ◆ tribes
- ◆ traditional methods

People and Places

- ◆ Sahara
- ◆ Red Sea
- ◆ North Africa
- ◆ sub-Saharan Africa
- ◆ Atlas Mountains
- ◆ Mount Kilimanjaro
- ◆ Great Rift Valley
- ◆ Nile River
- ◆ Niger River
- ◆ Congo River
- ◆ Zambezi River
- ◆ Arabs
- ◆ Egypt
- ◆ South Africa

The continent of Africa has a lot of diamonds and gold. Africa is rich in many natural resources. But it is also one of the poorest regions in the world.

Africa's Landforms

Africa is located between the Atlantic Ocean and the Indian Ocean. Africa has a long, smooth coast. There are not many harbors or ports. So it has been hard for Africans to use the seas for trading.

The Sahara, which means "desert," stretches from the Atlantic Ocean to the Red Sea. It is the world's largest desert. Years can pass without rain in the Sahara.

The Sahara divides Africa into two regions. North Africa includes the Sahara and the region south of the Mediterranean Sea. The rest of Africa is called sub-Saharan Africa, or Africa below the Sahara.

A huge plateau covers most of Africa. The plateau is higher in eastern and southern Africa. A narrow coastal plain surrounds the plateau. The Atlas Mountains are

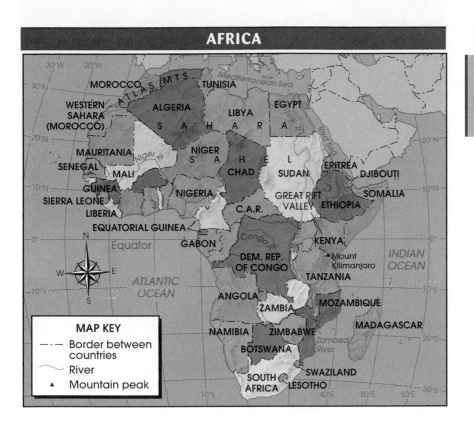

AFRICA

Africa has more nations than any other continent. What nation in Africa is also an island?

in northwest Africa. There are no mountain chains south of the Sahara. But there are some high mountains. The highest mountain in Africa is Mount Kilimanjaro. It is always covered with snow.

The Great Rift Valley is an important landform in east Africa. It runs north to south for more than 4,000 miles. The Great Rift Valley is made of deep, wide cracks in Earth's surface. Many lakes are in this valley.

Africa has four large rivers. The Nile River in east Africa is the longest river in the world. The Niger, Congo, and Zambezi rivers are other long African rivers. These rivers have many waterfalls. Waterfalls make it difficult to travel on the rivers. So it has been hard for Africans to travel and trade with each other. Waterpower from the rivers produces electricity.

The Great Rift Valley

Climate and Vegetation

Almost all of Africa lies in the tropics. But Africa has five climate regions. Each region has different **vegetation**, or plants such as trees, shrubs, and grass.

The region in central Africa near the Equator has a hot, wet tropical climate. There is heavy rain every day. Tropical rain forests grow in this climate. There

3

This part of the African savanna is called the Serengeti Plain.

is less rain as you move north or south away from the Equator. Areas at the Equator with high elevations have a cooler climate.

The second climate region is north and south of the rain forests. The climate is very hot, with both rainy and dry seasons. **Savannas** cover this region. Savannas are land areas with long, thick grass and short trees. Many wild animals live on the savannas.

North and south of the savannas, the climate is **semiarid**. It is still hot, but drier. There may be only ten inches of rain during the year. Short grasses grow in this third region. There are few trees. This semiarid region is part of the **Sahel**. The Sahel is a region of dry **grasslands** south of the Sahara. The Sahel stretches from the Atlantic Ocean to the Red Sea. Twelve countries are in the Sahel. The Sahel has long periods without rain called **droughts**. You will read more about this problem in Chapter 6.

The fourth region has a desert climate. The Sahara is north of the short grasslands. Smaller deserts are south of the southern grasslands at the southern end of Africa. The deserts have a few plants, but these plants need almost no water.

The fifth region has a Mediterranean climate. Summers are hot and dry. Winters are short and rainy. This climate is found in North Africa near the Mediterranean Sea. Grapes, olives, oranges, and other crops grow in this climate. This climate is also found at the southern tip of Africa.

The Sahel

Looking at North Africa

North Africa is the region that includes the Sahara and all the land north of it. North Africa has become very different from the rest of Africa. This is because the Sahara is so hard to cross. North Africa has the culture of the Middle East. Like the Middle East, most North Africans are Arabs. They speak the Arabic language. Most people are Muslims. Muslims follow the religion of Islam.

Egypt has the largest population in North Africa. It is one of the leaders of the Arab world. Most Egyptians live on the fertile land near the Nile River.

Oil is the most important resource in North Africa and the Middle East. You will learn more about North Africa and the Middle East in Unit 2.

Africa's History and Economy

People have lived in Africa for thousands of years. Early Africans did fine art work. They built large cities.

Hundreds of different ethnic groups have always lived in Africa. Usually these groups live together in close groups called **tribes**. Each ethnic group has its own language, religion, and culture.

From the 1800s to 1960, European countries ruled most of Africa. They wanted to own Africa's gold,

A mosque in Africa

The type of clothes that these women are wearing is part of their culture.

Sugarcane is an important crop in Egypt.

diamonds, copper, and other resources. Europeans divided most of Africa into colonies. Often Africans from different ethnic groups were forced to live together in one country. Many times these ethnic groups were enemies that could not get along. Today fighting between ethnic groups is still a big problem.

The Europeans needed modern transportation so they could mine Africa's resources. So they built roads, railroads, and seaports. They used these ports to ship minerals and raw materials to Europe. Raw materials are products from nature such as cotton, metal, and wood. They are used to make factory goods. Europeans often sold factory goods to their African colonies. Europeans also started plantations. They grew cash crops such as coffee, sugarcane, and cotton.

During the 1960s African nations began to rule themselves. They were no longer colonies. Now all African countries are independent.

Most Africans today earn a living by farming. They use **traditional methods** to grow crops. Most farmers use work animals to pull plows. They do not have modern farm machinery such as tractors. Farmers struggle to grow enough food for their families. Many people also raise sheep, goats, and cattle. Africans also work in mines. Africa exports its minerals to many nations. Each African nation earns most of its money by exporting only one or two farm or mineral products.

A gold mine in South Africa

Today all African countries except South Africa are developing nations. As you read this Unit, notice how Africans are working to improve their countries.

Chapter Main Ideas

1. The Sahara divides Africa into two regions. North Africa has the people and the culture of the Middle East. Sub-Saharan Africa is a poor region that has rich resources.

2. Most of Africa has a hot climate, but there is more rain as you get closer to the Equator.

3. Most African nations became independent countries during the 1960s. All are now independent.

◆ Vocabulary

Analogies Use the words in dark print that best complete the sentences.

savannas   Sahel   drought   traditional methods   vegetation

1. Too much rain is to flood as too little rain is to _____.

2. Birds and fish are to animal life as trees and grasses are to _____.

3. Very tall trees are to tropical rain forest as long grasses are to

_____.

4. Dry grasslands are to the _____ as rain forests are to tropics.

5. Heavy equipment is to modern technology as work animals are to

_____.

◆ Read and Remember

Finish the Paragraph Use the words in dark print to finish the paragraph below. Write the words you choose on the correct blank lines.

Equator   grasslands   waterfalls   Arab
Sahara   Sahel   Islam   plateau

The _____ divides Africa into two regions. North Africa

has the _____ culture of the Middle East. Most North Africans are

Muslims who follow the religion of _____. The area south of the

Sahara is the _____. It has dry _____. A large

_____ covers most of the African continent. African rivers

have _____ that make transportation by boat dangerous. Most

of Africa is hot. There is less and less rain as you move away from the

_____.

◆ Think and Apply

Cause and Effect Match each cause on the left with an effect on the right. Write the letter of the effect on the correct blank.

Cause

1. Africa's long, smooth coast does not have many harbors, so _____.

2. The hot land near the Equator gets lots of rain, so _____.

3. It is difficult to travel across the Sahara, so _____.

4. Desert covers most of Egypt, so _____.

5. European nations needed raw materials for their factories, so _____.

6. Europeans needed transportation in order to mine Africa's resources, so _____.

7. During the 1960s, most African nations became independent, so _____.

Effect

A. they started colonies in Africa

B. people live on fertile land near the Nile River

C. tropical rain forests grow in the region

D. they are no longer colonies

E. Africa does not have a lot of trade with other parts of the world

F. there are great differences between northern and southern Africa

G. they built roads and railroads

◆ Journal Writing

Imagine you are beginning a journey through Africa. Would you want to visit North Africa or Africa south of the Sahara? Write a paragraph in your journal telling which part of Africa you want to visit. Write two or more reasons to explain why you made this choice.

SKILL BUILDER

Reading a Vegetation Map

A **vegetation map** helps you learn which regions have different types of vegetation, or plant growth. Climate affects the type of vegetation that grows in a region. In Africa, vegetation changes where there is more rain or less rain. The map key tells you the color used on the map to show each type of vegetation.

Study the vegetation map and its map key on this page. Then finish each sentence in Group A with an answer from Group B. Write the letter of the correct answer on the blank line.

Group A

1. You can find Mediterranean vegetation in North Africa near the Mediterranean Sea and at the _____.

2. You will not find a tropical rain forest in _____.

3. The largest dry vegetation region in North Africa has _____.

4. You will find grasslands in a hot, rainy climate to the north and south of the _____.

5. East of the tropical rain forest at the Equator are grasslands in a _____.

6. Africa's smallest vegetation regions have _____ vegetation.

Group B

A. North Africa

B. tropical rain forest

C. hot, wet climate

D. Mediterranean

E. tip of South Africa

F. desert plants

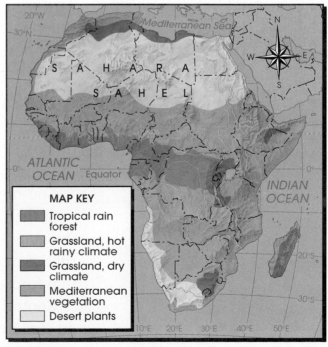

MAP KEY
- Tropical rain forest
- Grassland, hot rainy climate
- Grassland, dry climate
- Mediterranean vegetation
- Desert plants

Vegetation Map of Africa

CHAPTER 2

Nigeria: The Oil-Rich Nation of West Africa

Where Can You Find?

Where can you find a lake that was formed by building a dam on the Niger River?

Think About As You Read

1. How is southern Nigeria different from northern Nigeria?
2. How does Nigeria earn its money?
3. What problems are found in Lagos?

New Words

- swamps
- delta
- reservoir
- yams
- cassava
- assemble
- urbanization
- overcrowded

People and Places

Nigeria
Jos Plateau
Gulf of Guinea
Benue River
Kainji Lake
Lagos
Abuja
Kano
Hausas
Yorubas
Ibos

Nigeria is the only oil-rich country south of the Sahara. Nigeria also has more people than any other African country. About 104 million people live in Nigeria. Oil and a large population make Nigeria an important country. But it is still a developing country with millions of poor people.

Nigeria's Climates and Landforms

Nigeria is in western Africa. Much of Nigeria is on the Jos Plateau. Nigeria's southern coast is on the Gulf of Guinea. This gulf is part of the Atlantic Ocean.

Southern Nigeria has a hot, rainy tropical climate near the Equator. Coastal plains cover the land near the gulf. Farmers in the south grow cocoa beans, rubber trees, and palm trees. The area also has tropical rain forests and **swamps**. A swamp is soft, wet land.

Central Nigeria is in Africa's second climate region. Its climate is hot, with both wet and dry seasons. Savannas cover parts of central Nigeria.

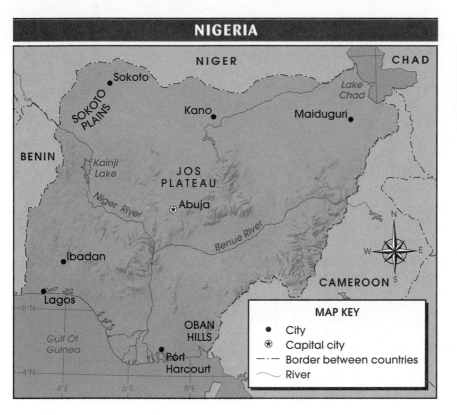

NIGERIA

Sokoto

SOKOTO PLAINS

NIGER

Kano

Maiduguri

CHAD

Lake Chad

BENIN

Kainji Lake

JOS PLATEAU

Niger River

Abuja

Benue River

Ibadan

N

W   E

S

CAMEROON

Lagos

6°N

Gulf Of Guinea

OBAN HILLS

Port Harcourt

4°N

4°E   6°E   8°E

MAP KEY
- • City
- ⊛ Capital city
- –·– Border between countries
- ～ River

The Benue and Niger rivers flow through Nigeria. Where is the delta of the Niger river located?

Nigeria's flag

Northern Nigeria is part of the Sahel. Some places get almost no rain. Dry grasslands cover the north. Farmers in the north grow cotton, sugarcane, peanuts, and wheat. They also raise cattle, sheep, and goats.

There are many rivers and streams in Nigeria. In central Nigeria the Benue River flows into the Niger River. The Niger is the third largest river in Africa. It flows from western Nigeria toward the center of the country. Then it flows south into the Gulf of Guinea. The Niger River forms a large **delta** near the Gulf of Guinea. A delta is land made of soil and sand that the river has carried and left at the place where the river flows into the sea. Nigeria's oil is found near the delta.

In the 1960s, Nigerians built a large dam on the Niger River. The dam stopped the river from causing dangerous floods. The dam used river water to produce lots of electricity. Water from the river was also used to make a new lake called Kainji Lake. Kainji Lake is a **reservoir**, a place that stores water for future use. People use Kainji Lake for fishing. They also use water from the lake to irrigate dry land so they can grow crops.

Traveling on a swamp in Nigeria

Nigeria exports oil all around the world.

Nigeria's Resources and Economy

Nigeria has coal, gold, iron, and tin. But oil is the country's most important resource. Oil was discovered in Nigeria in the 1960s. Nigeria sells oil to the United States and to many other countries.

Nigeria depends on selling oil to earn money. The country has problems when the price of oil goes down. That happened in the 1980s. Nigeria had to sell its oil for a lower price. The country earned much less money. Since then, the price of oil has gone up. About 90 percent of the country's money now comes from exporting oil. This money from oil has helped only a few Nigerians. Most people are very poor.

Most Nigerians are subsistence farmers. They eat rice, beans, corn, and **yams**. They also eat an African vegetable called **cassava**. Most Nigerians eat very little meat. Most farmers live in small villages and use traditional methods of farming. So they do not grow much food. The government is trying to use oil money to help farmers grow more food. It has bought better seeds and fertilizers. But the country still does not grow enough food for its people. So Nigeria imports a lot of food. But Nigeria does export some cash crops such as cocoa, cotton, rubber, peanuts, and palm oil.

Nigerians study better ways to grow cassavas.

Only one fourth of Nigeria's people live in cities. Lagos is the largest city. It has more than one million people. It is a port on the Gulf of Guinea. Lagos has many factories. Some of the factory products are cement, clothing, steel, and food products. Some factories also **assemble** cars and radios. Factory workers use parts that are made in other countries.

Lagos is a crowded city with big problems. Each year more poor farmers leave their villages and move to Lagos. They hope to find factory jobs there. This movement of people to cities is called **urbanization**. Poor people in Lagos live in slums. The city does not have enough clean water, schools, houses, jobs, or transportation. There is a lot of crime in Lagos.

At one time Lagos was the capital of Nigeria. In 1980 the government began to build a new capital in central Nigeria. The new capital is Abuja. It is not yet finished, so many government offices are still in Lagos. Kano is the largest city in the north. Most houses in Kano are made of baked mud. Long ago, Kano was a center of trade for people who had crossed the Sahara.

History, People, and Government

People have been living in Nigeria for more than 1,000 years. Most Nigerians belong to three large

Kano, Nigeria

Lagos used to be the capital of Nigeria. Lagos is a very crowded city.

For hundreds of years, the people of Nigeria have used mud bricks to build homes and other buildings.

School children in Nigeria

ethnic groups. In the north many people are Hausas. They follow the religion of Islam. In the South many people are Yorubas and Ibos. Most people in these groups are Christians.

There have been problems among the country's many ethnic groups. There are more than 250 different groups. Each group has its own culture and its own language. It is hard for Nigerians to feel that they are part of one country. It is hard to feel like one country because so many different languages are spoken. People from different groups also find it hard to work together to solve problems.

During the late 1800s, Great Britain began to rule Nigeria. In 1960, Nigeria became an independent country. The new government made English the official language. It is the language used in Nigerian schools.

Nigeria is not a democracy. An army dictator rules Nigeria. A small group of rich people control the country. People are arrested if they work against the government.

Nigeria has many problems today. The population is growing very fast. Cities are **overcrowded** because they have too many people. There are not enough doctors and hospitals. There are not enough schools, so only half of the people can read and write. Farmers do not grow enough food for all the people. Most people have a very low standard of living. The country earns lots of money from its oil, but that money has not helped most people. Nigeria's leaders must find new ways to use the money from oil to help the Nigerian people.

Chapter Main Ideas

1. Nigeria has a hot, wet climate in the south. Northern Nigeria is hot and dry.
2. Nigeria earns most of its money from exporting oil. But most Nigerians have a low standard of living.
3. Nigeria has more than 250 ethnic groups and languages. English is the official language.

◆ Vocabulary

Finish Up   Choose the word or words in dark print that best complete each sentence. Write the word or words on the correct blank line.

urbanization	cassava	reservoir
swamp	delta	overcrowded

1. A _____ is an area of soft, wet land.

2. A _____ is land made of soil and sand where a river flows into the sea.

3. A place where water is stored for future use is a _____.

4. A _____ is an African vegetable.

5. When many people move from villages to cities, there is _____.

6. Cities that have too many people are _____.

◆ Read and Remember

Where Am I?   Read each sentence. Then look at the words in dark print for the name of the place for each sentence. Write the name of the correct place on the blank after each sentence.

Lagos   Abuja   Kainji Lake   Kano   Niger River

1. "I am on the third largest river in Africa." _____

2. "I am fishing at a lake that was formed by a dam on the Niger River."

_____

3. "I am in Nigeria's southern port and largest city." _____

4. "I am in Nigeria's new capital." _____

5. "I am in a large city in northern Nigeria." _____

◆ Think and Apply

Find the Main Idea   Read the five sentences below. Choose the main idea and write it in the main idea box. Then find three sentences that support the main idea. Write them in the boxes of the main idea chart. There will be one sentence in the group that you will not use.

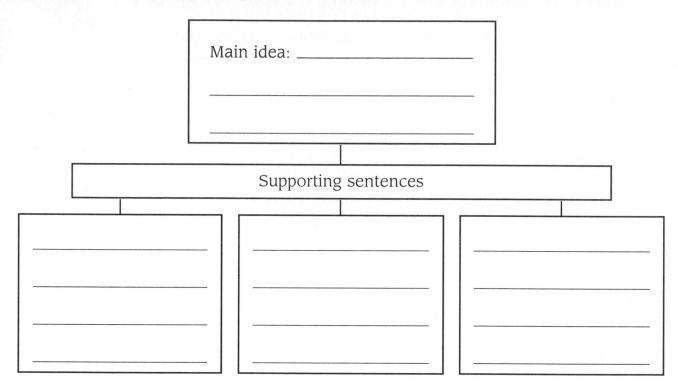

Main idea: _____

_____

_____

Supporting sentences

A. About half of Nigeria's people cannot read or write.

B. Most farmers use traditional methods.

C. English is Nigeria's official language.

D. Nigeria is a developing country with millions of poor people.

E. Only one fourth of the people live in cities.

◆ Journal Writing

Lagos has many problems because it is overcrowded. Write a paragraph that describes what Nigeria's government could do as it builds Abuja to avoid the problems it has in Lagos.

Reading a Climate Map

A **climate map** helps you learn about the weather in an area. It shows which places are rainy and which places are dry. A climate map helps you learn which places are hot and which are cooler. The map key on a climate map uses different colors to show different climates.

The map below shows the three climates found in Nigeria. As you travel from north to south in Nigeria, the climate becomes wetter.

Study the climate map. Then write the answer to each question.

1. What kind of climate does Lagos have? _____

2. What kind of climate is at the Niger River delta? _____

3. What climate does Abuja have ? _____

4. Is Kano's climate wetter or drier than that of Port Harcourt? _____

5. What two cities get less rain than Abuja? _____

6. What climate does Sokoto have? _____

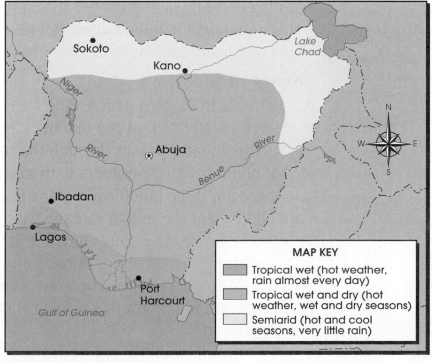

MAP KEY
- Tropical wet (hot weather, rain almost every day)
- Tropical wet and dry (hot weather, wet and dry seasons)
- Semiarid (hot and cool seasons, very little rain)

Climate Map of Nigeria

CHAPTER 3

Kenya: A Country in East Africa

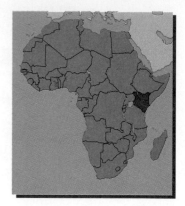

Where Can You Find?
Where can you find a huge lake with more than 200 kinds of fish?

Think About As You Read

1. What are Kenya's landforms and climates?
2. What products does Kenya export?
3. What is Kenya's biggest problem?

New Words

- ◆ nomads
- ◆ Swahili
- ◆ sisal
- ◆ wildlife
- ◆ national parks
- ◆ oil refineries

People and Places

- ◆ Kenya
- ◆ Mombasa
- ◆ Masai
- ◆ Mount Kenya
- ◆ Lake Victoria
- ◆ Kisumu
- ◆ Nairobi

Kenya is an African country that does not have silver or diamond mines. It does not have oil, coal, or iron. This nation has few resources. But Kenya has fertile land and beautiful places to visit.

Kenya's Landform Regions

Kenya is in eastern Africa. Find Kenya on the map on page 19. Notice that the Indian Ocean is to the east. The Equator passes through the middle of Kenya. What countries share borders with Kenya?

There are three landform regions in Kenya. There are plains near the Indian Ocean. These plains have a hot, wet climate. The soil is fertile and this region has some farming. Tropical rain forests and swamps are also in this plains region. There are beautiful beaches at the ocean. Mombasa is a busy port city on the Indian Ocean.

The second landform region is the plateaus that cover three fourths of Kenya. In most places these

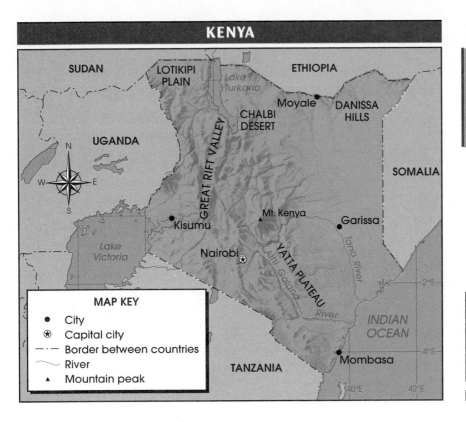

KENYA

SUDAN
LOTIKIPI PLAIN
Lake Turkana
ETHIOPIA
Moyale
DANISSA HILLS
CHALBI DESERT
UGANDA
GREAT RIFT VALLEY
SOMALIA
Mt. Kenya
Kisumu
Garissa
Tana River
Lake Victoria
Nairobi ⊛
YATTA PLATEAU
Athi Galana
River
INDIAN OCEAN
2°S
MAP KEY
• City
⊛ Capital city
–·– Border between countries
⁓ River
▲ Mountain peak
TANZANIA
Mombasa
4°S
40°E   42°E

Kenya is located in eastern Africa. Mount Kenya has the highest elevation in Kenya. What lake is located on Kenya's western border?

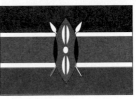

Kenya's flag

plateaus get little rain. Some plateaus are covered with savannas. A small group of Kenyans called the Masai are **nomads**. The Masai move across the plateaus herding cattle. Thousands of wild animals also live on Kenya's plateaus.

The highlands are the third landform region. Hills and mountains cover this land in southwest Kenya. Mount Kenya is in the highlands region. Mount Kenya is more than 17,000 feet high. It is located at the Equator. But snow and ice always cover the top of the mountain because of its high elevation.

The Great Rift Valley cuts through the highlands region. Many lakes are part of this valley. Part of Lake Victoria, Africa's largest lake, is on Kenya's border. People do a lot of fishing in this area. More than 200 kinds of fish live in this huge lake. Kisumu, Kenya's third largest city, is on Lake Victoria.

The high elevation of the highlands gives this region a mild climate. The land around Lake Victoria gets a lot of rain. There is enough rain for farming. The Great Rift Valley has very fertile soil. There are many farms in this region. So most of Kenya's people live in the

Masai herding cattle

19

Nairobi, Kenya

rural highlands. Nairobi, Kenya's capital and largest city, is in the highlands. About 2 million people live in Nairobi. This modern city is about one mile above sea level.

Kenya's History, People, and Culture

People have lived in Kenya for thousands of years. In 1895 Great Britain took control of Kenya. The British started large farms for growing tea and coffee. They also built a railroad across the country. That railroad made it possible to travel from Mombasa to Nairobi. From Nairobi you could travel by train to Lake Victoria. The railroad also connected Kenya with other African countries.

In the 1950s the people of Kenya began to fight for their freedom from Great Britain. In 1963 Kenya became an independent country. Kenyans wanted an African language as their official language. **Swahili** became the country's official language. English is the country's second official language.

Almost all Kenyans are black Africans. But Kenya has some Asians and whites. About three fourths of all Kenyans are Christians. Some people are Muslims. Many people follow traditional African religions.

About 28 million people live in Kenya. Most of them live in small villages. They belong to about 40 different ethnic groups. Each group has its own language and customs. Kenya's government has been trying to help the many groups get along. But in 1993 there was terrible fighting between a few groups. Thousands of people were killed.

A sisal plantation

Earning a Living and Protecting the Wildlife

Most Kenyans earn a living in one of three ways. Most people work at farming on small farms. They grow subsistence crops such as corn, cassava, rice, and beans. They do not use modern ways of farming. But there are also large tea and coffee plantations where modern methods are used. Kenya earns more money from exporting coffee than from any other product. Kenyans also grow and export cotton and **sisal**. Sisal is a plant that is used to make rope.

Tourists can see zebras and other animals in Kenya's national parks.

Tourism is the second way Kenyans earn money. Tourists from many parts of the world visit Kenya each year. Thousands of Kenyans work in tourist hotels and restaurants. Many tourists enjoy Kenya's beaches and cities. Some spend days climbing Mount Kenya.

Other tourists come to Kenya to see **wildlife**, or many kinds of wild animals. Kenya has large **national parks**, parks owned by the government, where wild animals are protected. These parks cover hundreds of miles of land. Hunting is not allowed in the parks. Tourists drive through these parks to watch and to photograph the wildlife. Elephants, zebras, lions, and giraffes can be seen in Kenya's national parks.

The third way Kenyans earn money is by making factory goods. Kenya is a developing country. Kenya still buys most of the factory goods it needs from Western Europe. But it is building many new factories. Today Kenya's factories make chemicals, clothing, food products, cement, and paper. Some factories assemble cars. Kenya also has **oil refineries**. In an oil refinery, oil is cleaned and made into different products such as motor oil and gasoline. Kenya does not have oil, so its refineries use oil from other countries.

Mount Kenya

Looking at Kenya's Future

Kenya has several problems. About half of the people are poor. They have a low standard of living.

Mombasa is Kenya's busiest port. It is located on the Indian Ocean.

Tourists in Kenya

Most people do not own a television, a telephone, or a car. Kenya's biggest problem is rapid population growth. This means the population is growing very fast. Most families have six or more children. Kenya has one of the fastest growing populations in the world. But only one fifth of the land can be farmed. It will be hard for Kenyans to grow enough food for many more people. The country will also need more jobs. These are important problems for Kenya.

Kenya is working on these problems. It now has more farms, factories, and tourists than ever before. Most people can read and write. Each year new schools are started. Now Kenya must try to solve the problem of rapid population growth. Then people will enjoy a higher standard of living.

Chapter Main Ideas

1. Most of Kenya's people live in the southwest highlands. The soil in this region is good for farming.
2. Coffee is Kenya's most important export. Kenyans work at farming, tourism, and factory jobs.
3. Kenya's biggest problem is rapid population growth. Kenya does not have enough fertile land to grow food for a larger population.

◆ Vocabulary

Finish the Paragraph   Use the words in dark print to finish the paragraph below. Write the words you choose on the correct blank lines.

sisal   **Swahili**   **national parks**   **oil refineries**   **nomads**

The Masai are _____ who move from place to place. They herd

cattle on Kenya's plateaus. Most people in Kenya live in the highlands. There they

grow a plant for making rope called _____. They also grow tea

and coffee. Kenyans speak an African language called _____.

Tourists enjoy seeing Kenya's wild animals in large _____ owned

by the government. Kenya has _____ where oil is cleaned so it can

be made into products.

◆ Read and Remember

Complete the Geography Organizer   Complete the geography organizer below with information about Kenya.

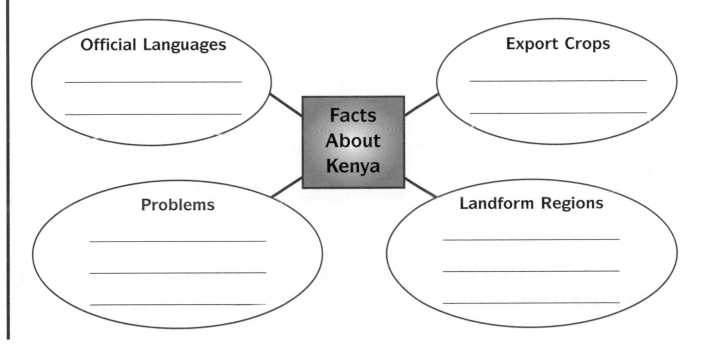

Find the Answer   Put a check (✓) next to each sentence that tells about a problem in Kenya. You should check three sentences.

_____ **1.** Many tourists visit Kenya each year.

_____ **2.** Kenya has few natural resources.

_____ **3.** The highlands have fertile soil.

_____ **4.** Kenya's population is growing very fast.

_____ **5.** Many people in Kenya are poor.

◆ Think and Apply

Compare and Contrast   Read each phrase below. Decide if it tells about Nigeria, Kenya, or both. Write the number of the phrase in the correct part of the Venn diagram.

1. East African country
2. oil is the main export
3. many ethnic groups
4. 104 million people
5. Great Rift Valley

6. coffee is the main export
7. West African country
8. became independent from Great Britain
9. developing country

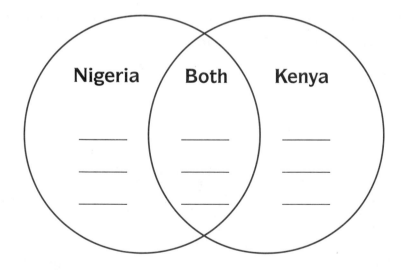

◆ Journal Writing

Write a paragraph in your journal that tells why rapid population growth is a big problem in Kenya.

Reviewing Line Graphs

The **line graph** on this page shows how Kenya's population has changed since 1970. A quick look at the graph tells you that the population has grown larger each year. Do you think Kenya's population next year will be larger than it is now?

Look at the graph on this page. Then finish each sentence in Group A with an answer from Group B. Write the letter of the correct answer on the blank line.

Group A

1. In 1970 Kenya's population was about _____.

2. In 1995 Kenya's population was about _____.

3. The graph does not show the year 1965. We can guess that

Kenya's population in 1965 was _____ than in 1970.

4. The smallest population change was between 1970 and _____.

5. We can guess that in the year 2000, Kenya's population will be

_____ than in 1995.

Group B

A. greater

B. smaller

C. 1975

D. 11 million

E. 28 million

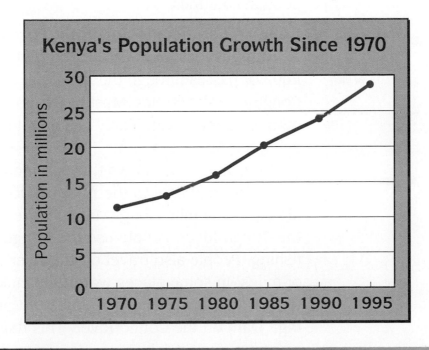

Kenya's Population Growth Since 1970

CHAPTER 4

Congo: The Largest Country in Central Africa

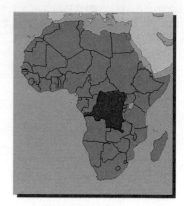

Where Can You Find?
Where can you find the world's longest lake?

Think About As You Read

1. How does the Congo River help Congo?
2. What problems are found in Congo's cities?
3. What resources are found in Congo?

New Words

- okapi
- Lingala
- malnutrition
- billionaire
- conflicts
- refugees
- rebelled

People and Places

Inga Dam
Congo Basin
Lake Tanganyika
Kinshasa
Belgian Congo
(Joseph) Mobutu Sese Seko
Laurent Kabila
Rwanda
Hutus
Tutsis

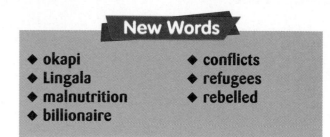

Congo should be one of the richest countries in Africa. It has lots of copper, diamonds, oil, and gold. Congo has rich resources. But it is one of Africa's poorest countries.

Congo's Landforms and Rain Forest

Congo is located in the central part of Africa. The Equator passes through the middle of Congo. All of Congo is in the tropics. Most of Congo is surrounded by other countries. Congo only has a 25-mile strip of land along the Atlantic Ocean.

The Congo River flows through most of the country. The river empties into the Atlantic Ocean. This river is almost 3,000 miles long. Many shorter rivers flow into the Congo River. People use the Congo River for fishing. People also travel on the river for hundreds of miles. In some places waterfalls make it impossible to travel on the river. The people of Congo built the Inga Dam on the Congo River. This dam makes large amounts of electricity.

DEMOCRATIC REPUBLIC OF CONGO

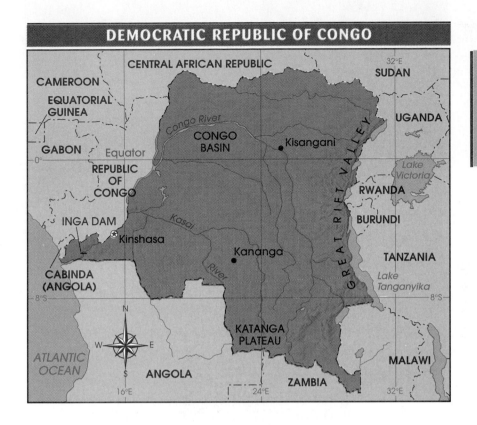

CENTRAL AFRICAN REPUBLIC
SUDAN
CAMEROON
EQUATORIAL GUINEA
UGANDA
GABON   Equator
CONGO BASIN
Kisangani
Congo River
Lake Victoria
REPUBLIC OF CONGO
RWANDA
INGA DAM
BURUNDI
Kasai
Kinshasa
Kananga
TANZANIA
River
Lake Tanganyika
CABINDA (ANGOLA)
GREAT RIFT VALLEY
KATANGA PLATEAU
ATLANTIC OCEAN
N W E S
ANGOLA
ZAMBIA
MALAWI
16°E   24°E   32°E

Congo is the largest country in central Africa. The Equator passes through this country. What city in Congo is located near the Equator?

The Congo Basin surrounds the Congo River. A basin is an area of land that is lower than the land around it. The Congo Basin is on a large plateau. A huge tropical rain forest covers much of the Congo Basin. This rain forest is the largest in Africa. Its trees are so thick and tall that the sun never reaches the floor of the forest. Thousands of different plants and animals live in the rain forest. The **okapi** is a furry animal that lives only in Congo's rain forests. It does not live in any other part of the world. The okapi is the symbol of Congo.

Congo's rain forest is being destroyed. People chop down trees to clear the land for farming. Trees from the forest are made into furniture and paper. People around the world want Congo to protect its rain forest from deforestation.

A plateau covers most of the land south of the Equator. Savannas cover this plateau. The climate is warm and rainy, but there is a dry season. The east and southeast have highlands. Hills and mountains cover this region. These highlands are part of the Great Rift Valley. Lake Tanganyika is in the Great Rift

An okapi

Kinshasa is a port on the Congo River.

Some people in Congo earn a living by fishing.

Valley on Congo's eastern border. It is the world's longest lake. It is more than 400 miles long.

Congo's People and Cities

About 47 million people live in Congo. Most of the people of Congo are black Africans. About 80 percent are Christians. Congo has more than 200 ethnic groups and about 200 different languages. French is Congo's official language. **Lingala** and Swahili are African languages that many people use.

About 40 percent of the people live in cities. Kinshasa is the capital and largest city. It has almost 5 million people. It is on the Congo River.

Congo's cities have many problems. There are few jobs, so unemployment is a big problem. Cities have no buses or trains. There are not enough schools or hospitals. Poor people live in terrible slums. Congo's cities are also dangerous because there is lots of crime.

Many Resources But a Low Standard of Living

Congo has many minerals. It earns most of its money by exporting minerals. Its most important exports are copper and diamonds. Congo also has oil, gold, tin, silver, and cobalt. The country also exports some cash crops. Coffee, cocoa, tea, and cotton are sold to other countries.

Most people in Congo live in small rural villages. Their standard of living is very low. Most villages do not have even one car, television, or telephone. Few homes have running water or electricity. Most people are struggling subsistence farmers who use hand tools. Their main foods are corn, rice, and cassava. Many people suffer from **malnutrition** because they do not get enough to eat. Malnutrition is poor health that is caused by a lack of healthy food.

Although most people in Congo are poor, many children in Congo go to school. Most schools have few books and supplies.

Congo's History

In 1885 the central part of Africa became a colony of Belgium. Belgium is a small country in Europe. This colony was called the Belgian Congo. It included land that would later become Congo. Belgium earned a lot of money from mining the colony's metals and minerals. The Belgians built cities, schools, railroads, churches, and hospitals. They also brought their French language to the colony.

The Africans living in the Belgian Congo wanted to rule themselves. In 1960 the colony became a free nation. Then it was called the Congo. Today the country is called the Democratic Republic of the Congo. Most of the time it is just called Congo. Between 1960 and 1965, different people in Congo fought to win control of their new country. Finally in 1965 an army general named Joseph Mobutu became the president of most of Congo. He ruled as a dictator until 1997. During that time, Congo became a very poor country. It became poor because Mobutu stole his country's money and minerals. Mobutu became a **billionaire**.

Conflicts, or fights, between ethnic groups have always been a problem in Congo. In 1994 that problem grew worse when two ethnic groups began fighting in Rwanda. Rwanda is Congo's eastern neighbor. The two groups, the Hutus and the Tutsis, fought a war. During the war the Hutus murdered at least 500,000 Tutsi people. The war ended when the Tutsis won control of the government. Many Hutus left Rwanda. They became **refugees** in eastern Congo. Refugees are people who leave their country during a war.

A village in Congo

A rebel soldier in Congo during the civil war

29

Many people left Rwanda and became refugees in Congo.

Laurent Kabila

These refugees encouraged Congo's Hutus and Tutsis to fight against each other.

In 1996 fighting among ethnic groups became a civil war in Congo. Millions of people were unhappy with Mobutu. Laurent Kabila became the leader of a civil war against him. The Tutsis were the largest group that **rebelled**, or fought against, Mobutu. The Hutus fought for Mobutu during the civil war. In 1997, after seven months of fighting, Kabila and the rebels won.

After the civil war, Kabila became president of Congo. He promised to improve the country's standard of living and help it become a democracy. But in 1997 Kabila said it was against the law to protest against the government. People could not join political parties. Many people wonder if Congo will improve without Mobutu. Will Congo use its resources to raise its standard of living? Will the country become a democracy? No one knows what the future of this mineral-rich country will be.

Chapter Main Ideas

1. Savannas cover the southern part of Congo. Northern Congo has a large tropical rain forest that is being destroyed.
2. From 1965 to 1997 President Mobutu ruled Congo as a dictator.
3. Laurent Kabila led Tutsi rebels against Mobutu and the Hutus during a civil war. The rebels won and Kabila became the new president.

◆ Vocabulary

Find the Meaning   Choose the word or words that best complete each sentence. Write the words on the blank lines.

1. A **basin** is land that is surrounded by _____ land.

    lower   drier   higher

2. An **okapi** is a _____ that lives only in Congo.

    furry animal   fish   large cat

3. **Lingala** is an African _____.

    town   city   language

4. **Malnutrition** means people have poor health because they do not get enough

  _____.

    clothing   food   money

5. A **conflict** is a _____.

    fight   mountain   culture

6. A **refugee** is a person who moves to another country because of a _____.

    job   party   war

7. When people **rebelled**, they _____ against their government.

    spoke   fought   wrote

◆ Read and Remember

Write the Answer   Write one or more sentences to answer each question.

1. How do people use the Congo River? _____

_____

2. What is happening to Congo's tropical rain forest? _____

_____

3. What problems are found in Congo's cities? _____

_____

4. What problems do people in Congo have because of the low standard of living?

_____

5. Which ethnic group won the civil war in Rwanda? _____

_____

6. Why did Tutsis begin fighting against Congo's army in 1996? _____

_____

7. Who became president when the civil war ended in 1997? _____

_____

◆ Think and Apply

Sequencing Write the numbers **1, 2, 3, 4,** and **5** next to these sentences to show the correct order.

_____ In 1994 Hutus in Rwanda killed thousands of Tutsis.

_____ The rebels led by Laurent Kabila won the civil war.

_____ Joseph Mobutu became the leader of Congo.

_____ Fighting between Congo's Hutus and Tutsis led to civil war in Congo in 1996.

_____ The Tutsis won control of Rwanda's government, so Hutu refugees went
        to Congo.

◆ Journal Writing

Write a paragraph in your journal that tells why Congo has a low standard of living even though it is rich in resources.

CHAPTER 5

The Republic of South Africa

Where Can You Find?

Where can you find a mountain that has a flat top like a table?

Think About As You Read

1. What are South Africa's three landforms?
2. How is South Africa different from other African countries?
3. How has South Africa changed since 1990?

New Words

- cape
- escarpments
- apartheid
- racial groups
- minority
- coloreds

People and Places

- Cape Agulhas
- Cape Town
- Cape of Good Hope
- Table Mountain
- Lesotho
- Orange River
- Dutch
- Cape Colony
- Nelson Mandela
- F.W. de Klerk

The Republic of South Africa is very different from other African countries. It is not in the tropics. Fewer than half of the people are farmers. It is a rich industrial country with many kinds of factories. South Africa is the only developed country in Africa.

Geography, Climate, and Cities

South Africa is located on the southern tip of the continent. The place that is farthest south is named Cape Agulhas. A **cape** is a point of land that sticks out into a large body of water. The Atlantic Ocean is to the west of this cape. The Indian Ocean is to the east. South Africa has a long coast with beautiful beaches. There are large ports on the coast. These ports help South Africa trade with other countries. Cape Town is a large port city on the Atlantic Ocean side of the Cape of Good Hope. Table Mountain is a famous place in Cape Town. The top of this mountain is flat like a table.

Lesotho is surrounded by South Africa. South Africa has three capital cities. Each one has a different part of the government. What are South Africa's capital cities?

SOUTH AFRICA AND LESOTHO

MAP KEY
- • City
- ⊛ Capital city
- –·– Border between countries
- ⌇ River
- ▲ Mountain peak

South Africa's flag

Escarpments in South Africa

South Africa has three main landforms. It has a narrow coastal plain. North of the coastal plain are mountains and **escarpments**. Escarpments are steep cliffs. The highest mountains in this region are in Lesotho. Lesotho is a small country surrounded by the country of South Africa. The third landform is a large plateau north of the mountains. This plateau covers most of South Africa. The plateau is covered with grasslands.

The Orange River is the longest river in South Africa. It flows into the Atlantic Ocean. There are several other long rivers. South African rivers have many waterfalls. So the rivers cannot be used for shipping and transportation.

Most of South Africa has a warm, sunny climate. There is not much rain. The climate becomes drier as you travel west. There are deserts in the west and in the northwest.

South Africa is south of the Equator. So it is in the Southern Hemisphere. In the Southern Hemisphere the seasons are the opposite of those in the Northern Hemisphere. In South Africa winter is in June and July.

At least half of South Africa's people live in modern cities. These cities have many industries. They have good roads and public transportation.

History, People, and Apartheid

The first people to live in South Africa were black Africans. Then in the 1600s, the Dutch came to southern Africa from Europe. They settled in the region and called it Cape Colony. Later people from Great Britain settled in the region. During the early 1900s, the British won control of the region and changed its name to South Africa. In 1931 South Africa became an independent country. White South Africans won control of the country's government.

In 1948 the South African government passed **apartheid** laws. These laws allowed white people to control the country's government, natural resources, and money. The government divided the country's people into four **racial groups**. The circle graph on this page shows these groups. Whites are a **minority**, a small part of the population. **Coloreds** are people who have black and white or black and Asian parents. The laws kept the racial groups apart. Each group had its own schools and hospitals. Under apartheid only whites could vote.

Black South Africans and many whites worked to end apartheid laws. One black leader, Nelson Mandela, spent many years in jail because of his work to end apartheid. Finally in 1990 South Africa's president, F.W. de Klerk, began ending these laws. In 1991 all of the apartheid laws ended.

In 1994 South Africa held free elections. For the first time, people from all racial groups could vote. Some people waited in line for many hours to vote. Nelson Mandela became the country's first black president.

Today all South Africans have equal rights. Whites no longer control the government. But white people still have a much higher standard of living.

Resources and Economy

South Africa is very rich in natural resources. The country earns most of its money from exporting

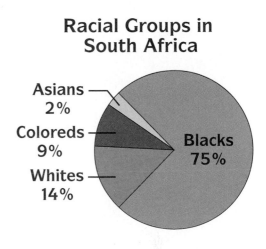

Racial Groups in South Africa

Asians 2%
Coloreds 9%
Whites 14%
Blacks 75%

F.W. de Klerk

Many people in South Africa still have a low standard of living.

New neighborhoods in South Africa give people better places to live.

minerals. Most of the world's gold and diamonds come from South Africa. This country also has coal, iron, copper, silver, and other metals. It has fish from its oceans. There are many kinds of wildlife. But South Africa must buy oil from other countries.

South Africa has more factories than any other African country. South Africans make most of the products they need in their factories. The country imports technology from Western Europe, Asia, and the United States.

Only about one third of all South Africans work at agriculture. Many people also raise sheep and cattle. The country grows most of the food it needs. It exports sugar, fruit, and wine. It also exports lots of wool.

There are big differences between white and black farmers. White farmers have large farms and modern farm machines. They grow cash crops. Most blacks are subsistence farmers. They grow their crops on small farms. They do not have modern farm machines.

South Africa earns more than one billion dollars each year from tourism. Many people enjoy visiting the country's huge national parks. There they can see elephants, lions, monkeys, and other types of wildlife.

Working for a Better South Africa

One of South Africa's biggest problems is that blacks, coloreds, and Asians have a much lower standard of living than white people. Their standard of living is lower because apartheid laws allowed whites to control South Africa's money and resources for many years.

Today almost half of all blacks do not have jobs. Many blacks are homeless. Others live in city slums or small village huts. Malnutrition is a problem because many people do not have enough food.

South Africans can solve these problems by working together. They have already changed their country into a democracy where all people have equal rights. Now they must find ways to raise the standard of living.

Table Mountain in Cape Town

Chapter Main Ideas

1. South Africa is Africa's only developed country.
2. South Africa earns most of its money by exporting gold, diamonds, and other minerals. It also exports food, wool, and wine.
3. In 1994 all racial groups voted in the first free elections. Nelson Mandela became South Africa's president.

BIOGRAPHY

Nelson Mandela (Born 1918)

Nelson Mandela worked to end South Africa's apartheid laws. Mandela is a lawyer who became a leader of the African National Congress. This group worked for equal rights for all racial groups. Mandela was arrested for his work to end apartheid. He spent 27 years in prison. During that time his wife Winnie and other people in many nations worked to help him win freedom. He became one of the world's most famous prisoners. At last in 1990, President F.W. de Klerk allowed Mandela to be free.

After leaving prison, Mandela worked with President de Klerk to end apartheid. In 1993 both men received the Nobel Peace Prize for their work. After South Africa's first free elections in 1994, Mandela became the country's first black president.

Journal Writing
Write a paragraph in your journal about Nelson Mandela. Tell how he helped South Africa.

◆ Vocabulary

Finish Up   Choose the word or words in dark print that best complete each sentence. Write the word or words on the correct blank line.

coloreds	**racial groups**	**escarpments**
cape	**minority**	**apartheid**

1. A _____ is a point of land that sticks into a large body of water.

2. Steep cliffs are called _____.

3. Blacks, whites, and Asians are three of South Africa's _____.

4. A group of people that is less than half of the population is a _____.

5. People in South Africa with white and black parents or Asian and black parents

   are _____.

6. South African laws that kept racial groups apart were called

   _____ laws.

◆ Read and Remember

Write the Answer   Write one or more sentences to answer each question.

1. What kind of climate does South Africa have? _____

   _____

2. What country does South Africa surround? _____

3. How do climates differ in the Northern and Southern Hemispheres?

   _____

4. What did the apartheid laws do? _____

   _____

5. What event happened in South Africa in 1994? _____

_____

6. How does South Africa earn money? _____

_____

7. Why do tourists visit South Africa? _____

_____

◆ Think and Apply

Categories   Read the words in each group. Decide how they are alike.
Find the best title for each group from the words in dark print. Write the title
on the line above each group.

People Who Settled in South Africa   **South African Resources**
Problems of Black South Africans   **South African Landforms**
Changes in South Africa   **Southern Hemisphere**

1. _____   **4.** _____
escarpments   black Africans
plateau   Dutch
coastal plain   British

2. _____   **5.** _____
gold and diamonds   malnutrition
coal and iron   low standard of living
fish and wildlife   subsistence farming

3. _____   **6.** _____
the end of apartheid laws   winter in June and July
all racial groups could vote   summer in December and January
Nelson Mandela became president   south of the Equator

◆ Journal Writing

Write a paragraph in your journal that tells how South Africa has changed
since 1990. Tell about three or more changes.

Reading a Population Map

A **population map** shows where people in a region live. It also can show which areas are densely populated and which areas have a lower population density. It can also show the population density of cities. The map key helps you learn the population of a region.

Look at the population map of South Africa. Then finish each sentence in Group A with an answer from Group B. Write the letter of each correct answer on the blank line.

Group A

1. _____ is a port with fewer than one million people.

2. A southeastern port with more than one million people is _____.

3. There are _____ cities in South Africa with more than 5 million people.

4. In the region around Lesotho, there are _____ people per square mile.

5. The deserts have _____ people per square mile.

6. _____ is a city in central South Africa with fewer than one million people.

7. We can conclude from the map that there is greater population density in the _____.

Group B

A. no

B. 25–100

C. east

D. Kimberly

E. Durban

F. Port Elizabeth

G. 0–25

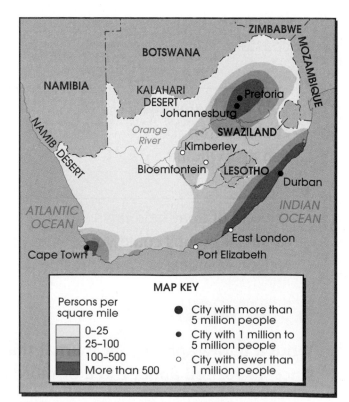

Population Map of South Africa

CHAPTER 6

Working for a Better Africa

Where Can You Find?
Where can you find two countries that have planted many new trees?

Think About As You Read

1. What are some serious problems in Africa today?
2. What are the causes of hunger in Africa?
3. How are Africans trying to solve their problems?

New Words

- ◆ hunger
- ◆ famine
- ◆ desertification
- ◆ overgraze
- ◆ erosion
- ◆ disease
- ◆ tsetse fly
- ◆ AIDS
- ◆ foreign aid
- ◆ experts
- ◆ loans
- ◆ United Nations
- ◆ Peace Corps
- ◆ gorge

People and Places

- ◆ Ethiopia
- ◆ Somalia
- ◆ Victoria Falls
- ◆ Zambia
- ◆ Zimbabwe

Snow-covered mountains, tall waterfalls, sandy beaches, and interesting wildlife make Africa a beautiful continent. It is also rich in natural resources. But Africa is also the poorest region in the world. Africans must solve five big problems so that people can have a higher standard of living.

Rapid Population Growth and Hunger

Africans must solve the problems of **hunger** and rapid population growth. The population is growing faster in Africa than in any other part of the world. African governments cannot provide enough food, jobs, and services for all their people. To solve this problem, people must learn to have smaller families.

Hunger is Africa's second problem. Africa does not grow enough food for its people. Africans grew less food in the 1990s than they did in the 1970s. Hunger leads to malnutrition and poor health.

Many people in Africa have starved during famines.

Many people in Africa continue to use traditional methods of farming.

There are many causes of hunger. **Famine** is one cause. A famine is a terrible shortage of food for a long period of time. Droughts, long periods without rain, often cause famine. Africa has had many droughts. Droughts have caused many famines in Ethiopia. During these famines, millions of people have starved. Developed nations usually send food to help countries that have famines.

A second cause of hunger is that many farmers use traditional methods of farming. They do not have modern machines, good seeds, or good fertilizers. A third cause is that too many farmers grow cash crops such as coffee and cotton. Not enough farmers grow crops Africans can eat.

The fourth cause of hunger is civil wars. Soldiers burn or destroy the crops of their enemies. This happened during the 1992 civil war in Somalia in east Africa. A fifth cause is poor transportation. There are not enough roads, trucks, or trains, so farmers cannot send their crops to the people in cities and villages.

Desertification

Desertification is a third problem in Africa. Desertification means grasslands become smaller and deserts grow larger. Africa's huge Sahara is spreading into the Sahel. So there is less land for growing food. Desertification happens when farmers allow their sheep and cattle to **overgraze**. This means sheep and cattle eat all the grasses and their roots. Then there is no grass to hold down the soil. Without grass the land turns into desert.

Deforestation also causes deserts to grow larger. Deforestation means forests in a region are destroyed. This happens when people chop down too many trees. Without trees there is **erosion**. This means soil is blown away by wind or is washed away by rain. Then the land turns into desert.

Africans are working to stop desertification. In Kenya and in Ethiopia, people are planting many new trees. The new trees prevent erosion. They stop the land from becoming desert.

Illiteracy and Disease

Many people in Africa cannot read a newspaper. Illiteracy, not knowing how to read or write, is Africa's fourth problem. For example, in Ethiopia only one third of the people can read and write. In South Africa many black adults do not know how to read. To solve this problem, governments are building new schools and training more teachers.

When these trees are larger, they will be planted in a forest in Kenya.

Cattle and other animals have overgrazed some land in Africa.

A tsetse fly

Disease, or sickness, is the fifth problem. Insects spread many kinds of diseases throughout Africa. One serious disease is the "sleeping sickness." It is spread by the **tsetse fly**. Africans also become sick from drinking water that is contaminated. **AIDS** is the most serious disease in Africa today. AIDS is spreading fast, and people die from the disease. There is no cure for AIDS yet. But people all over the world are looking for a cure and for better ways to protect people from disease.

Working for a Better Africa

Africans are working to solve their problems. To solve the hunger problem, people are trying to grow more food. In some places people are learning to use modern farming methods and better seeds, fertilizers, and tools. They are also learning better methods to irrigate dry land.

African governments are trying to start new industries and use modern technology. New factories are being built in Africa's cities. Then countries have more products that they can export to earn money. They do not have to depend on one or two cash crops or minerals to earn money.

Foreign aid is helping African nations. Foreign aid is money and help that developed nations give to developing counties. African nations use foreign aid to build dams, roads, factories, and schools. Most African countries receive foreign aid. Foreign aid also means sending **experts** to teach Africans better ways to farm and use their resources. Health experts teach people how to prevent and treat diseases.

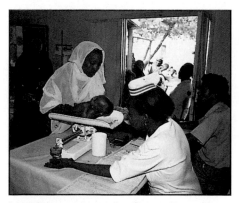
Health experts in Somalia

Sometimes foreign aid is money that one nation lends another. Then African nations must repay the **loans**. Poor countries find it very hard to repay loans. Many countries now have debts that they cannot repay.

Sometimes foreign aid is given to African countries during a famine. In 1992 Somalia had a famine and a civil war. More than a million people were starving. Thousands of American soldiers were sent to Somalia. They helped the **United Nations**, or UN, deliver food

Millions of people starve when there are civil wars.

to starving people. The UN is an organization of countries that work together. The soldiers stayed and helped the people of Somalia for more than a year.

Some Americans are helping Africa by joining the **Peace Corps**. The Peace Corps is an American group that sends its members to help developing countries. In Africa, Peace Corps members start schools. They teach Africans better ways to farm. Other developed countries also send people to Africa to do the same kind of work that Peace Corps members do. They teach Africans how to help themselves.

Africa's people are working to solve their problems. Countries are starting new industries. People are learning better ways to grow food. More children are going to school. People are learning about health care. They are trying to destroy dangerous insects. Africa is slowly becoming a better place to live.

Developed countries send food to countries that have famines.

Chapter Main Ideas

1. Africa's biggest problems are rapid population growth, hunger, desertification, illiteracy, and disease.
2. Millions of Africans have starved during famines.
3. African nations receive foreign aid from the United States and other developed countries.

Victoria Falls

Victoria Falls is one of the world's largest waterfalls. It is more than 300 feet high and more than one mile wide. The falls are located on the border between the countries of Zambia and Zimbabwe. Victoria Falls is formed by the flow of water from the Zambezi River over a high **gorge**. A gorge is a deep valley with steep rocky walls. The river is one mile wide where it flows over the gorge. As the river flows down into the gorge, it sprays huge amounts of water into the air. That spray looks like smoke. It can be seen forty miles from the falls. The sprayed water allows a rain forest to grow near the falls. The falling water sounds like loud thunder. Long ago, Africans called the falls, "smoke that thunders." There is often a rainbow in the sky above the falls.

A dam located near the falls uses waterpower to make electricity for people in the region. A railroad bridge crosses Victoria Falls. That bridge allows people to go across the falls from Zambia to Zimbabwe. People can walk across the bridge. Or they can travel by car or train on the bridge.

Victoria Falls is a wonderful tourist region with many hotels. People who want adventure can go rafting in the gorge below the falls. Other tourists fly over the falls in small airplanes. At night tourists can watch shows with traditional African dancing. All tourists need raincoats at the falls because the spray from the falls makes clothing very wet.

Victoria Falls

Write a sentence to answer each question.

1. **Location**   Where is Victoria Falls?

_____

2. **Human/Environment Interaction**   How does the dam near the falls help

   people? _____

3. **Movement**   How can people go across Victoria Falls from Zambia to

   Zimbabwe? _____

◆ Vocabulary

Match Up   Finish the sentences in Group A with words from Group B. Write the letter of each correct answer on the blank line.

Group A

1. When a region does not have food for a long period of time, there is a _____.

2. When grasslands become deserts, there is _____.

3. When cattle eat all the grass in a region, they have _____.

4. When people get sick, there is _____.

5. The money and help that developed nations give to developing countries is called _____.

Group B

A. foreign aid

B. disease

C. overgrazed

D. desertification

E. famine

◆ Read and Remember

Find the Answer   Put a check (✓) next to each sentence that tells how people are working to solve Africa's problems. You should check four sentences.

_____ 1. In Ethiopia people have planted many trees.

_____ 2. Many hungry people have malnutrition.

_____ 3. Families have many children.

_____ 4. African governments are building schools and training teachers.

_____ 5. Africans are building new factories.

_____ 6. In some countries many people cannot read or write.

_____ 7. Foreign aid money is used to build dams, roads, factories, and schools.

◆ Think and Apply

Drawing Conclusions   Read each pair of sentences. Then look in the box for the conclusion you might make. Write the letter of the conclusion on the blank.

1. The population is growing faster in Africa than in any other region in the world. African governments cannot provide food and services for all the people.

   Conclusion: _____

2. African farmers cannot grow enough food because of droughts and civil wars. Farmers grow cash crops like cotton instead of growing food people can eat.

   Conclusion: _____

3. Overgrazing kills all the grass of the grasslands, leaving the ground bare. Erosion occurs when forests are destroyed.

   Conclusion: _____

4. Only one third of the people of Ethiopia can read.
   Africa needs more schools and teachers.

   Conclusion: _____

5. Many people in Africa have AIDS.
   Insects spread disease and people get sick from drinking contaminated water.

   Conclusion: _____

Conclusions
   A. Illiteracy is a problem in Africa.
   B. African deserts are growing larger because of desertification.
   C. Rapid population growth is a problem in Africa.
   D. There are many causes of hunger.
   E. Disease is a problem in Africa.

◆ Journal Writing

Write a paragraph about two serious problems in Africa today. Tell one or two ways each problem can be solved.

The Middle East

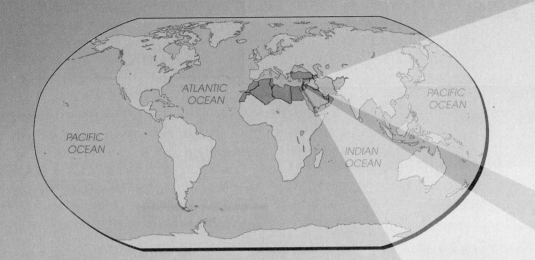

Damascus, Syria

The Dead Sea

DID YOU KNOW?

▲ Damascus, the capital of Syria, is the world's oldest capital city.

▲ Egypt was one of the first places in the world to have tourists. More than 2,000 years ago, Greeks and Romans came to see Egypt's tombs and temples.

▲ The Dead Sea is a saltwater lake that has the saltiest water in the world. The water is almost ten times saltier than regular ocean water.

▲ Turkey was the first Muslim country in the Middle East to have a woman as its prime minister.

WRITE A TRAVELOGUE

The Middle East and North Africa have deserts, oil fields, cities, and villages. Look at the photographs of the region in this unit. Choose two different types of places you would like to visit. Write a paragraph in your travelogue that tells why those two places interest you. After reading the unit, choose two other places in different countries that you might want to visit. Tell what is special about those places.

THEME: PLACE

CHAPTER 7

Looking at the Middle East

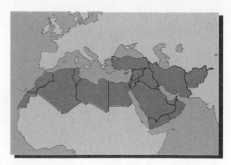

Where Can You Find?
Where can you find a capital city built at a large oasis?

Think About As You Read

1. Why is the Middle East a crossroads region?
2. What resource is very scarce in the Middle East?
3. What religions began in the Middle East?

New Words

◆ crossroads
◆ oasis
◆ steppe climate
◆ monotheism
◆ Judaism
◆ Christianity
◆ Koran
◆ Hebrew
◆ phosphates

People and Places

◆ Bedouins
◆ Middle East
◆ Persian Gulf
◆ Saudi Arabia
◆ Riyadh
◆ Tigris River
◆ Euphrates River
◆ Israel
◆ Jesus
◆ Muhammad
◆ Iran
◆ Lebanon

It is late at night in the desert. A tired young man rests in his tent. He rode a camel for many hours in the hot desert sun. He worked hard taking care of his family's sheep and goats. Tomorrow the man and his family will move again. They are Bedouins. About one million Bedouins live in the deserts of the Middle East. They are nomads who move from place to place in the desert.

The Region and Its Geography

The Middle East is a region that includes countries in southwestern Asia and northern Africa. About 350 million people live in this part of the world. Sometimes people use the name Middle East just for the countries in southwestern Asia. As you read this unit, you will find that some countries in northern Africa share the same culture as the countries in southwestern Asia.

The Middle East is often called a **crossroads** region. It is a crossroads because people often pass

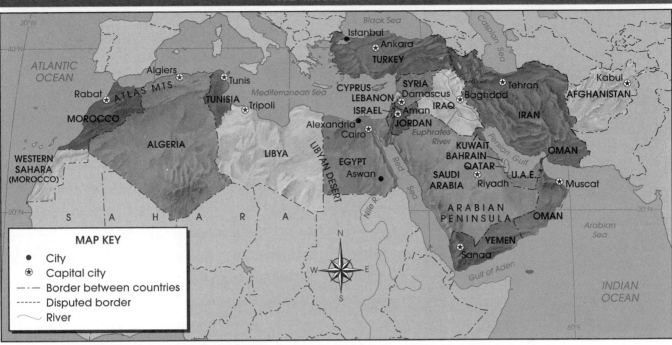

ATLANTIC OCEAN

Algiers

Rabat ⊛ ATLAS MTS. ⊛ Tunis

MOROCCO TUNISIA ⊛ Tripoli

ALGERIA LIBYA

WESTERN SAHARA (MOROCCO)

S A H A R A

Black Sea

Istanbul ● ⊛ Ankara

TURKEY

CYPRUS SYRIA
LEBANON Damascus
ISRAEL ⊛ Aman IRAQ

Alexandria ● JORDAN Euphrates River
Cairo ●

LIBYAN DESERT EGYPT Aswan ●

Mediterranean Sea

Tehran ●
Baghdad

IRAN

Kabul ●
AFGHANISTAN

KUWAIT
BAHRAIN
QATAR
SAUDI ⊛ U.A.E.
ARABIA Riyadh

OMAN

⊛ Muscat

ARABIAN PENINSULA OMAN

YEMEN
⊛ Sanaa

Arabian Sea

Gulf of Aden

INDIAN OCEAN

Caspian Sea

Red Sea

Nile R.

Persian Gulf

MAP KEY
● City
⊛ Capital city
–·– Border between countries
----- Disputed border
~ River

The Middle East is a region that includes countries in southwestern Asia and northern Africa. Which countries are in northern Africa?

through the Middle East to travel between Europe, Asia, and Africa.

Three important bodies of water are found in the Middle East. They are the Mediterranean Sea, the Persian Gulf, and the Red Sea. These seas are used for shipping, trade, and transportation from one continent to another.

There are several different kinds of landforms in the Middle East. There are lowland plains near the coasts. Hills, mountains, and valleys cover many areas away from the coasts. Plateaus also cover parts of the Middle East.

Climates and Rivers

Water is scarce everywhere in the Middle East. It is one of the driest regions in the world. Deserts cover more than half of the region. The huge Sahara Desert covers most of North Africa. A large desert covers most of Saudi Arabia. There are deserts in the northeastern part of the region, too.

A camel market

Because there is water at oases, people can live and farm in the desert.

While traveling through a desert, you might suddenly come to a place with grass and trees. You would be at an **oasis**. An oasis is a place in the desert that has underground water. Many people in the Middle East live near oases and raise sheep, goats, and crops. Riyadh, the capital of Saudi Arabia, was built at a large oasis.

The Middle East has three climates. Most of the region has a desert climate. Areas that are near the Mediterranean Sea have short, rainy winters and long, dry summers. They enjoy a Mediterranean climate. Other areas have a **steppe climate**. A steppe climate has small amounts of rain during the year. Grasses grow in a steppe climate.

Riyadh, Saudi Arabia

Because there is so little rain, millions of people in the region live near rivers. The Nile, the Tigris, and the Euphrates rivers have been important for more than 5,000 years. The soil near these rivers is fertile. People can farm because they use river water to irrigate their fields. Thousands of years ago, people built the world's first cities near these rivers.

Religion and People of the Middle East

Three of the world's important religions began in the Middle East. The three religions teach **monotheism**, a belief in one God. **Judaism**, the religion of the Jews, is the oldest of the three religions. It began in Israel thousands of years ago.

Christianity, the Christian religion, developed from Judaism. This religion follows the teachings of Jesus. Jesus was a Jew who lived about 2,000 years ago. Christians believe that Jesus was the son of God.

Islam began in Saudi Arabia in the year 622. It was started by an Arab leader named Muhammad. He taught that there is one God. Muslims believe that Muhammad was God's messenger. Muhammad's teachings are in the **Koran**. This book is holy to Muslims. The language of the Koran is Arabic. You will learn more about Islam in Chapter 11.

Who are the people of the Middle East? Most people are Arabs. They speak Arabic. In Turkey and Iran the people are Muslims but they are not Arabs. Today 90 percent of the people in the Middle East are Muslims. Some countries, such as Lebanon and Israel, have a small Christian population. In Israel most people are Jews. Their language is **Hebrew**.

A page from the Koran

Resources and Earning a Living

Oil is the region's most important natural resource. There is more oil in this region than in any other part of the world. Many developed nations do not have enough oil. So they buy oil from the Middle East. Oil-rich countries, such as Saudi Arabia and Iran, earn most of their money by exporting oil.

Studying the Koran

In Israel, road signs are written in Hebrew, Arabic, and English.

These phosphates will be exported to countries around the world.

This region has a few other resources. Some countries have natural gas. Some have iron ore. A few countries have **phosphates**. Phosphates are used in fertilizers.

More than half of the people in the Middle East earn a living by farming. The region has millions of farmers, but most of the land is too dry for farming. Most farmers in the Middle East do not use modern machines and methods. They work the same way farmers worked hundreds of years ago. Israel is one of the few countries in the region where farmers use modern methods.

Most nations in the Middle East are developing countries. Some countries are using the money they earn from selling oil to develop new industries. The standard of living in most of this region is much lower than the standard of living in Western Europe or the United States. Only a small part of the population does factory work.

Most people in the Middle East are poor. Most countries do not grow enough food to feed their people. Wars have been a problem in this region for thousands of years. Today this region still does not have real peace. In the next chapters, find out how people live in four countries of this region.

Chapter Main Ideas

1. The Middle East is the driest region in the world. Most people live near seas or rivers.
2. Judaism, Christianity, and Islam began in the Middle East.
3. Arabs are the largest ethnic group in the Middle East. Most people in this region believe in Islam.

◆ Vocabulary

Finish the Paragraph   Use the words in dark print to finish the paragraph below. Write the words you choose on the correct blank lines.

monotheism   **Koran**   **Christianity**   **steppe climate**
crossroads   **oasis**   **Judaism**

The Middle East is a _____ region because people often pass

through it to travel between Europe, Asia, and Africa. The Middle East is a dry

region. Some places have a _____ because they get small

amounts of rain during the year. In the desert, water can be found at an

_____. Three religions of the Middle East teach people to believe

in one God. This belief is called _____. The religion of the

Jews is _____. People who follow the teachings of Jesus believe

in _____. The teachings of Islam are in a book called the

_____.

◆ Read and Remember

Write the Answer   Write one or more sentences to answer each question.

1. Where is the Middle East? _____

_____

2. What three bodies of water are in the Middle East? _____

_____

3. What are three types of climates in the Middle East? _____

_____

4. What are three important rivers in the Middle East? _____

_____

5. What three religions began in the Middle East? _____

_____

6. What are some of the teachings of Islam? _____

_____

7. What is the most important resource in the Middle East? _____

_____

8. Why is only a small amount of land in the Middle East good for farming?

_____

◆ Think and Apply

Fact or Opinion Write **F** next to each fact below. Write **O** next to each opinion. You should find four sentences that are opinions.

_____ **1.** The Mediterranean Sea is to the north of North Africa.

_____ **2.** More people should live near the Nile River.

_____ **3.** People in the Middle East use river water to irrigate their farms.

_____ **4.** It is better to live near an oasis than to live near a river.

_____ **5.** Monotheism began in the Middle East.

_____ **6.** Most people in the Middle East believe in Islam.

_____ **7.** The people of the Middle East should export more phosphates.

_____ **8.** Nations that have oil should lower the price of oil.

◆ Journal Writing

Imagine living in the Middle East. Would you want to be a Bedouin, a farmer, or a city worker? Write a paragraph in your journal that tells which way of life you would want and why.

CHAPTER 8

Egypt: The Gift of the Nile

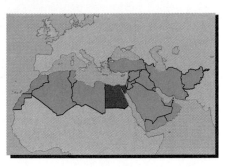

Where Can You Find?
Where can you find the only subway system in Africa?

Think About As You Read

1. How are the nations of North Africa alike?
2. How does the Nile River help Egypt?
3. How has the Aswan High Dam helped and hurt Egypt?

New Words

- Islamic fundamentalism
- deposited
- silt
- chemical fertilizers
- ancient
- pharaohs
- pyramids
- manganese
- unfavorable balance of trade

People and Places

- Morocco
- Algeria
- Tunisia
- Libya
- Sinai Peninsula
- Suez Canal
- Nile Delta
- Nile Valley
- Egyptians
- Aswan High Dam
- Lake Nasser
- Alexandria

For 5,000 years the people of Egypt have lived on land near the Nile River. The Nile River is just as important to Egypt today as it was long ago.

The Region of North Africa

Egypt has the largest population in North Africa. Morocco, Algeria, Tunisia, and Libya are other nations in the region. The Sahara Desert covers most of these countries. Most people in this region live near the Mediterranean Sea. People in Egypt also live along the Nile River. The Nile is the only long river in North Africa. North Africans use the Mediterranean Sea to trade with Europe and other parts of the Middle East.

All North African countries are developing nations. Most people work as subsistence farmers. Algeria and Libya have rich oil resources. These countries are using the money they earn from selling oil to become more developed.

The only long river in North Africa is in Egypt. What is the name of the river?

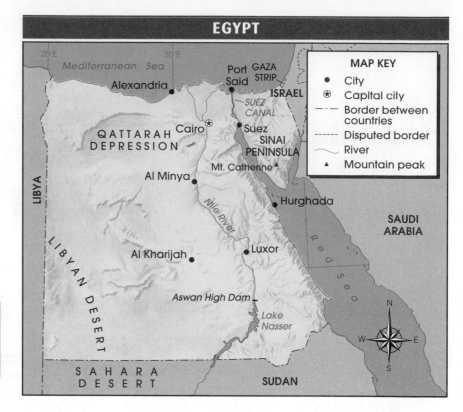

EGYPT

MAP KEY
- • City
- ⊛ Capital city
- — · — Border between countries
- ------ Disputed border
- ∿ River
- ▲ Mountain peak

Egypt's flag

The Suez Canal

In all of the countries in North Africa, most people are Arabs. The official language is Arabic. Their religion is Islam.

A movement called **Islamic fundamentalism** is changing North Africa and other countries in the Middle East. This means many Muslims have turned away from western values. Instead they follow the strictest rules of Islam. Because of Islamic fundamentalism, more people are wearing traditional Muslim clothing. Sometimes the leaders of this movement force people to follow the ways of Islam. When this happens there is less freedom.

Egypt: Climate, Landforms, and the Suez Canal

Egypt is in the northeastern part of North Africa. The country has a hot, dry climate. Deserts cover most land west and east of the Nile River. Deserts also cover the Sinai Peninsula. The Sinai Peninsula is part of eastern Egypt. Rocky hills are part of the Sinai and the eastern desert. A large plateau covers most of western Egypt.

Egypt earns large amounts of money from ships that use the Suez Canal. The canal allows ships to sail between the Mediterranean Sea and the Red Sea. Ships from many nations use the Suez Canal. The canal makes it faster to sail from Europe to Asia. Ships pay money to Egypt to use the canal.

The Nile River and the Aswan High Dam

The Nile is Egypt's only river. It is more than 4,000 miles long. It begins far from Egypt in central Africa near the Equator. The Nile flows from south to north. In the North, at the mouth of the river, the Nile empties into the Mediterranean Sea. For thousands of years, the river has **deposited** soil at the mouth of the river. This soil built up and formed a delta. The Nile Delta has very fertile soil.

Egypt is called the "Gift of the Nile." It has this name because the waters of the Nile and the fertile soil have been used to grow crops on dry desert land. The land around the Nile is called the Nile Valley. Every summer, for thousands of years, the river flooded the Nile Valley. The flood waters left **silt** on the land around the river. Silt is tiny pieces of soil. The silt made the Nile Valley very fertile. For thousands of years, people have farmed the Nile Valley. For thousands of years, people have used Nile water to irrigate farms in the Nile Valley.

The Nile Valley and the Nile Delta have less than five percent of Egypt's land. But most of Egypt's people live on this land. Most of Egypt's cities are in the Nile Valley.

Between 1960 and 1968, Egyptians built a huge dam on the Nile River. It is called the Aswan High Dam. The

The Nile Delta seen from outer space

Silt from the Nile River made the Nile Valley very fertile.

The water from Lake Nasser irrigates fields in the Nile Valley all year long.

The Aswan High Dam

dam stopped the floods of the Nile River. It has helped Egypt in several ways. The dam saves the Nile's water in a large lake, or reservoir, called Lake Nasser. Water from the reservoir is used to irrigate fields all year long. Egypt now has much more farmland. Egyptians grow twice as much food as they did before 1968. The dam also uses waterpower to make large amounts of electricity.

But the Aswan High Dam has also caused four problems. First, the Nile Valley no longer has floods from the river. So the Nile Valley no longer gets new silt from the river. The soil is less fertile. Farmers must use **chemical fertilizers** on the soil. Many poor farmers do not have enough money to buy these fertilizers. Second, chemical fertilizers have polluted the Mediterranean Sea. The fertilizers have killed some of the fish in the sea. Third, erosion is a problem at the Nile Delta. The delta no longer gets new soil each year. The waves of the Mediterranean Sea are washing away land at the mouth of the river. Fourth, tiny snails that carry disease now live all year in Lake Nasser. People who swim, bathe, or wash clothes in the lake water can become very sick.

Egypt's History, People, and Cities

Egypt's history began more than 5,000 years ago. People farmed the Nile Valley. They built cities near the Nile. Egyptians traded with countries around the Mediterranean Sea.

Ancient Egypt was ruled by kings called **pharaohs**. Some of the pharaohs forced slaves to build huge **pyramids** in the desert. The pharaohs were buried in these pyramids when they died. Many pyramids are still standing today.

Today Egypt is the largest Arab country in the Middle East. About 60 million people now live in Egypt. It is one of the leaders in the Arab world. More Arabic books and movies are made in Egypt than in any other country.

One of Egypt's pyramids

Egypt has a population that is growing very fast. About half of the people live in cities. Cairo is Egypt's largest city. It is on the Nile River in northern Egypt. Cairo is more than 1,000 years old. About 10 million people live in and around the city. There are modern hotels, homes, and office buildings. Cairo has the only subway system in all of Africa. But Cairo has millions of poor people. They live in tiny apartments. They do not have electricity or running water in their homes.

Cairo is on the Nile River.

Alexandria is Egypt's second largest city. It is a large port on the Mediterranean Sea.

Resources and Economy

Egypt's most important resource is oil. Egypt exports its oil to Europe and the United States. It also has iron ore, **manganese**, and coal.

Almost half of the people earn a living by farming. Cotton is the main cash crop. Egypt also exports large amounts of dates. Farmers grow sugarcane, rice, wheat, and oranges. But they do not use modern methods. Egypt must import half of the food it needs.

Egypt earns more than a billion dollars each year from tourism. Tourists visit Egypt's pyramids and museums. They also enjoy boat trips on the Nile.

Some Egyptians do factory work. Egyptian factories make cloth, food products, and other goods. Egypt has an **unfavorable balance of trade**. This means Egypt buys more goods from other countries than it exports. The United States has given Egypt billions of dollars in foreign aid.

Today Egypt has a low standard of living. Cities are very crowded. Millions of people are very poor. The country needs more farmland and more factories. Egyptians are trying to solve these problems. They want their country to continue to be a great leader in the Arab world.

Chapter Main Ideas

1. The countries of North Africa are developing nations. Most people are Arabs and believe in Islam.
2. Egypt is the "Gift of the Nile." The Nile allows people to grow food in the desert near the river.
3. The Aswan High Dam has given Egypt farmland and electricity. But the dam has caused erosion of the Nile Delta and has harmed fish in the Mediterranean Sea.

Cutting sugarcane

A street in Alexandria

◆ Vocabulary

Finish Up   Choose the word or words in dark print that best complete each sentence. Write the word or words on the correct blank line.

pharaohs	**pyramids**	**unfavorable balance of trade**
silt	**ancient**	**Islamic fundamentalism**

1. A return to the strict rules of Islam is _____.

2. The floods of the Nile River left soil called _____ on the land around the river.

3. The history of _____ Egypt began 5,000 years ago.

4. Long ago the kings of Egypt were called _____.

5. Thousands of years ago, Egyptian kings were buried in _____.

6. When a nation imports more than it exports, it has an _____.

◆ Read and Remember

Where Am I?   Read each sentence. Then look at the words in dark print for the name of the place for each sentence. Write the name of the correct place on the blank after each sentence.

Alexandria   Nile Valley   Lake Nasser   Sinai   Cairo   Nile Delta

1. "I am on a peninsula in eastern Egypt." _____

2. "I am on land formed by the build up of soil at the mouth of the Nile River."

_____

3. "I am on the fertile land around the Nile River." _____

4. "I am at a huge lake made by the Aswan High Dam." _____

5. "I am in the largest city on the Nile River." _____

6. "I am at a large port on the Mediterranean Sea." _____

Write the Answer   Write one or more sentences to answer each question.

1. Why is Egypt the "Gift of the Nile"? _____

_____

2. How has the Aswan High Dam helped Egypt? _____

_____

3. How has the Aswan High Dam hurt Egypt? _____

_____

4. What are Egypt's resources? _____

_____

◆ Think and Apply

Categories   Read the words in each group. Decide how they are alike.
Find the best title for each group from the words in dark print. Write the title
on the line above each group.

Suez Canal   Aswan High Dam   North African Nations   Nile River

1. _____

mostly desert
most people are Muslim Arabs
the most people live near the
   Mediterranean Sea

2. _____

makes electricity
holds water in Lake Nasser
stops floods of the Nile River

3. _____

waterway joins Mediterranean and
   Red seas
ships sail between Europe and Asia
Egypt earns money

4. _____

starts near the Equator
more than 4,000 miles long
empties into the Mediterranean Sea

◆ Journal Writing

Imagine that you are a tourist in Egypt. Write a paragraph in your journal that
tells about three or more places you would want to visit. Tell why you would
visit those places.

Reviewing a Resource Map

The **resource map** on this page shows where Egypt's important minerals and crops are found. Use the map key to find out which resources are shown. Then circle the word or words that best complete each sentence.

1. A food crop that is found at oases in the desert is _____.

dates   cotton   rice

2. Two mineral resources in the Sinai Peninsula are _____.

coal and iron   gold and phosphate

oil and manganese

3. Two important minerals in northern Egypt are _____.

coal and gold   oil and natural gas

manganese and phosphate

4. A food crop near Luxor is _____.

wheat   corn   rice

5. An important cash crop near Luxor is _____.

rice   corn   cotton

6. There are _____ food crops in the Sinai Peninsula.

no   a few   many

7. A food crop that grows in the Nile Delta is _____.

dates   rice   apples

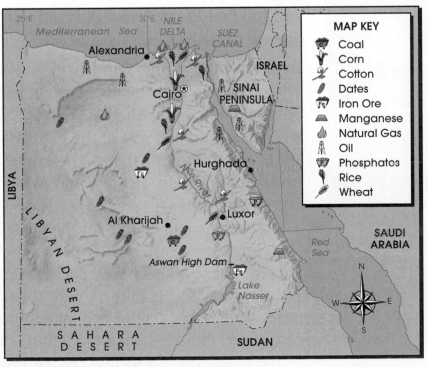

Resource Map of Egypt

CHAPTER 9

Israel: A Jewish Country

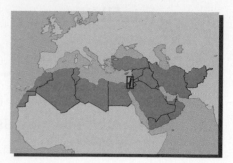

Where Can You Find?
Where can you find the lowest spot on Earth?

Think About As You Read

1. How is Israel different from other countries in the Middle East?
2. How do Israelis grow food in the desert?
3. How did Israel become a Jewish country?

New Words

- scarce
- drip irrigation
- kibbutz
- software
- homeland
- Palestinian Liberation Organization (PLO)

People and Places

- Israelis
- Negev Desert
- Sea of Galilee
- Dead Sea
- Jerusalem
- Tel Aviv
- Beersheba
- Palestinians
- Jordan
- Old City
- Gihon Spring

Where can you find the lowest spot on Earth? Where can you find the only Jewish country in the world? The answer to both questions is Israel.

Israel's People and Landforms

More than 5 million people live in Israel. The people of Israel are Israelis. About 83 percent of Israelis are Jews. Arabs are the rest of the population. The Arabs are Muslims and Christians. The laws of Israel allow freedom of religion. Hebrew and Arabic are the two official languages of Israel.

Israel is a small country at the eastern end of the Mediterranean Sea. There are coastal plains near the sea. These plains have beaches, farms, and cities. The Negev Desert is in the south. Hills cover northern Israel. The Sea of Galilee is a lake in the north. Pipes carry water from this lake to all parts of Israel.

The Dead Sea is a saltwater lake in Israel. It is part of the Great Rift Valley. The Dead Sea is the lowest

ISRAEL

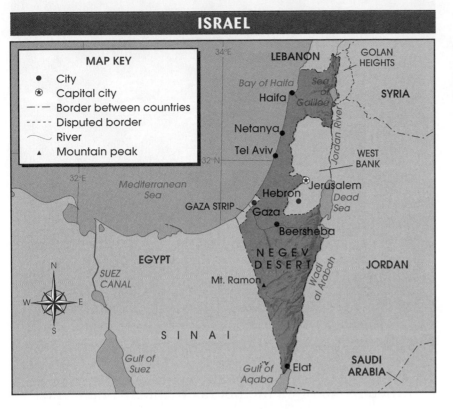

MAP KEY
- • City
- ⊛ Capital city
- –·– Border between countries
- ---- Disputed border
- ∼ River
- ▲ Mountain peak

34°E
LEBANON
GOLAN HEIGHTS
Bay of Haifa
Sea of Galilee
Haifa
SYRIA
Netanya
Jordan River
Tel Aviv
32°N
WEST BANK
32°E
Mediterranean Sea
Jerusalem
Hebron
Dead Sea
GAZA STRIP
Gaza
Beersheba
EGYPT
NEGEV DESERT
JORDAN
SUEZ CANAL
Mt. Ramon
Wadi al Arabah
SINAI
Gulf of Suez
Gulf of Aqaba
Elat
SAUDI ARABIA

Deserts cover more than half of the Middle East. What large desert is found in Israel?

Israel's flag

spot on Earth. Its water is so salty that no plants or fish can live in the Dead Sea.

Cities and Farms

Most Israelis live in cities. Jerusalem is the capital and the largest city. It is Israel's center of government and culture. Tel Aviv is a large city on the Mediterranean coast. It is the country's center of business and industry. Beersheba is the largest city in the Negev. The city began thousands of years ago near an oasis.

Only five percent of Israelis are farmers. They use modern machines and lots of fertilizer. They grow most of the food Israel needs. Israel exports food, wine, and flowers to many nations.

Israelis know how to grow food in the desert. They have built pipelines to carry water from the Sea of Galilee to the Negev. Water is **scarce**, so Israelis are careful not to waste it. They use a method called **drip irrigation**. This means hoses carry water to each plant. Each plant gets just enough water to grow. Israeli farmers are teaching people in developing countries better ways to grow food.

Drip irrigation in the Negev

A kibbutz on the Sea of Galilee

This fruit grows on a kibbutz.

Many farms in Israel are **kibbutz** farms. A kibbutz is owned by all of its members. Members share the work on the kibbutz. They do not get paid. But the kibbutz gives its members all the things they need. There are schools and doctors. Members eat together in a large dining room. A kibbutz may have a hotel where tourists can stay during a vacation. Only a small part of Israel's people live on kibbutz farms. But these people grow a lot of Israel's food.

Resources, Economy, and Government

Israel has very few resources. There is no coal, oil, waterpower, natural gas, or iron ore. The nation mines salt and minerals from the Dead Sea and the Negev. Israel must import most raw materials that it needs for its industries.

Israel must import oil and coal to produce electricity. But Israel has plenty of sunlight. Almost every Israeli house uses solar energy, or energy from the sun, to make hot water.

Israel is a developed country. All children go to school for many years. Most Israelis work at service jobs. Many service jobs are in the tourist industry. About one fifth of the people have factory jobs. Some Israeli factory products are computer **software**, food products, clothing, and weapons. Israeli diamond cutters make more polished diamonds than any other country. Israel does not earn enough money because it has an unfavorable balance of trade. It imports many more products than it exports.

Israel is a democracy. All citizens, Arabs and Jews, can vote. Citizens vote for members of Parliament. A prime minister leads the country.

Israel's History and Problems

Thousands of years ago, the Jews ruled Israel. They believed God gave the land of Israel to their people. Later the land was conquered by other peoples. Most of the Jews were forced to move to other countries. But some Jews have always lived in Israel. Many Arabs came to live in the region when the Jews left.

During the late 1800s, Jews began to move back. They wanted to make the region a Jewish **homeland** again. During World War II, millions of Jews were killed during the Holocaust. After the war many Jews wanted Israel to be their home again. In 1948 the United Nations formed the country of Israel.

A large group of Arabs left Israel when the new Jewish country was formed. These Arabs are called Palestinians. The Palestinians later wanted the area back. Since 1948 there has been fighting between Israelis and Palestinians over the land.

The people who live in this building use solar energy to make hot water.

Near downtown Tel Aviv

An Israeli soldier

These people from Ethiopia are new immigrants to Israel.

Fighting and wars have been a big problem for Israel. Since 1948 neighboring Arab countries have fought four wars against Israel. Each time Israel remained free. Israel still has some of the land that it took from these Arab countries during a war in 1967.

In 1979 Egypt became the first Arab country to sign a peace treaty with Israel. Israel returned to Egypt some of the land it had captured in 1967. In 1994 Jordan and Israel also signed a peace treaty. Other Arab countries refuse to make peace with Israel.

The Palestinians formed an organization called the **Palestinian Liberation Organization**, or PLO. The Israelis and the PLO have agreed to allow Palestinians to rule themselves in some of the areas that Israel captured in 1967. Some Israelis fear the PLO wants to rule all of Israel. Other people hope the Israelis and the Palestinians will live together peacefully.

Terrorism has been a problem in Israel. Arab terrorists have attacked buses, stores, and schools. A few Jewish terrorists have attacked Arabs. Many people have been killed.

Because of the wars, Israel has a large army. All men and women must serve in the army. Israelis pay very high taxes in order to pay for their army.

Jews from every part of the world have moved to Israel. Since 1980 starving Jews from Ethiopia have escaped to Israel. Thousands of Russian Jews have also made Israel their home. Israelis are working hard to give homes and jobs to the new immigrants.

Every year tourists visit Israel. They visit holy places in Jerusalem. They swim in the Dead Sea. Tourists enjoy this modern country in the Middle East.

Chapter Main Ideas

1. Israel is a developed country. Farmers use modern methods to grow most of the country's food.
2. Israel has few natural resources. It imports raw materials to make factory products.
3. Israel has fought and survived four wars since 1948.

Jerusalem

Jerusalem is a city that is holy to Jews, Christians, and Muslims. Jerusalem is located in central Israel. It has a cooler climate than cities on the coast because of its higher elevation.

Three thousand years ago, King David, the king of Israel, made Jerusalem the capital of his country. Large Jewish temples were built in the city. Walls were built around Jerusalem to keep out enemies. The oldest part of Jerusalem still has walls around it. This area is now called the Old City. Newer areas surround the Old City.

Water has always been scarce in Jerusalem. Long ago, people in Jerusalem got their water from the nearby Gihon Spring. The people were afraid that they might not be allowed to leave the city to get water during a war. So they built an underground tunnel. It went from the Old City to the Gihon Spring. That tunnel saved the people of Jerusalem during many wars.

Today Jerusalem is a region of culture and education. The city is famous for its museums, schools, and large university. Tourists from every part of the world visit its holy places and museums. Some tourists get their feet wet in the ancient tunnel leading to the Gihon Spring. Then they can return to their hotel to swim in a modern pool.

The Old City in Jerusalem

Write a sentence to answer each question.

1. Location   What is the location of Jerusalem?

_____

2. Place   Why is Jerusalem a special place?

_____

3. Movement   Why do tourists come to Jerusalem?

_____

◆ Vocabulary

Match Up   Finish the sentences in Group A with words from Group B. Write the letter of each correct answer on the blank line.

Group A

1. When there is not enough water, water is

   _____.

2. When hoses bring just enough water to

   each plant, there is _____.

3. A farm where people share the work and

   are given everything they need is a_____.

4. Programs that are made for a computer are

   _____.

5. A country that is home for a group of people

   is a _____.

6. An organization that wants a country for

   Palestinians is the _____.

Group B

A. homeland

B. drip irrigation

C. Palestinian Liberation Organization

D. scarce

E. software

F. kibbutz

◆ Read and Remember

Finish Up   Choose the word or words in dark print that best complete each sentence. Write the word or words on the correct blank line.

| Tel Aviv | homeland | Sea of Galilee | terrorists |
| imports | Jordan | Dead Sea | |

1. Pipes carry water from the _____ to all parts of Israel.

2. The lowest spot on Earth is at the _____.

3. A city on the Mediterranean Sea with lots of businesses and factories is

_____.

4. Israel _____ raw materials for its industries.

5. Israel was created to be a Jewish _____ after the Holocaust.

6. Egypt and _____ are the only Arab countries that have signed peace treaties with Israel.

7. Israeli buses, stores, and schools have been attacked by _____.

◆ Think and Apply

Finding Relevant Information   Imagine you are telling your friend why Israel is a developed country. Read each sentence below. Decide which sentences are relevant to what you will say. Put a check (✔) in front of the relevant sentences. You should find six relevant sentences.

_____ **1.** Israel uses solar energy to make hot water.

_____ **2.** Most people work at service jobs.

_____ **3.** A small group of farmers grow most of the country's food.

_____ **4.** Israel is a democracy with a Parliament.

_____ **5.** Israel imports the oil it needs.

_____ **6.** Israeli factories make computer software.

_____ **7.** Jewish immigrants from many countries have moved to Israel.

_____ **8.** Israel gets some minerals from the Dead Sea.

_____ **9.** Israeli farmers use modern machines and fertilizer.

_____ **10.** Most people live in cities.

◆ Journal Writing

Write a paragraph in your journal that tells three ways in which Israel is different from other countries in the Middle East.

Comparing a Climate Map With a Population Map

By comparing a **climate map** with a **population map**, you can learn about a region. The population map on this page shows us that southern Israel has a much lower population density than northern Israel. The climate map shows us that southern Israel has a desert climate. So we can conclude that the south has fewer people because of its desert climate.

Study the map keys on both maps. Then use the words in dark print to finish each sentence.

500–1,500   4   Sea of Galilee   Mediterranean   Beersheba

1. All of the cities near the _____ have fewer than 100,000 people.

2. Israel has a higher population density where there is a _____ climate.

3. The only city with a desert climate that has population of more than 100,000 is

   _____ .

4. There are _____ cities on the Mediterranean Sea that have more than 100,000 people.

5. The region around Herzliya has _____ people per square mile.

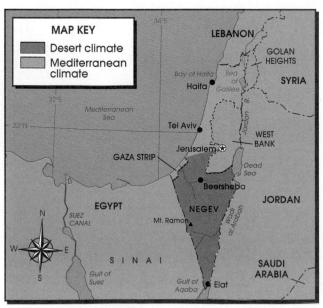

Climate Map of Israel

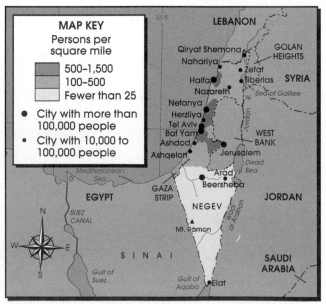

Population Map of Israel

CHAPTER 10

Turkey: A Country on Two Continents

Where Can You Find?
Where can you find a city with bridges that connect Europe with Asia?

Think About As You Read

1. Why does Turkey have ties to both Europe and the Middle East?
2. What are Turkey's landforms and climates?
3. How did Mustafa Kemal Ataturk change Turkey?

New Words

◆ strait
◆ Ottoman Empire
◆ secular
◆ shish kebab
◆ chromite

People and Places

◆ Bosporus Strait
◆ Thrace
◆ Anatolia
◆ Turks
◆ Ottoman Turks
◆ Mustafa Kemal Ataturk
◆ Kurds
◆ Istanbul
◆ Constantinople
◆ Hagia Sofia
◆ Ankara

Turkey is the only country in the Middle East with land in both Europe and Asia. The people of Turkey have ties to both regions.

Turkey's Landforms, Climate, and Resources

Turkey is a country on two continents. The Bosporus Strait separates the European part of Turkey from the Asian part. A **strait** is a narrow body of water that connects two larger bodies of water. Ships can sail from the Black Sea through the Bosporus Strait. From there they sail into the Mediterranean Sea.

The European part of Turkey has fertile hills and plains. This part of the country is called Thrace. Most of Turkey is in Asia. The Asian part of Turkey is called Anatolia. Anatolia has coastal plains in the north and south. Most of Anatolia is covered with a large dry plateau. High mountains surround the plateau.

People enjoy a Mediterranean climate near the Black and Mediterranean seas. Turkey's mountains

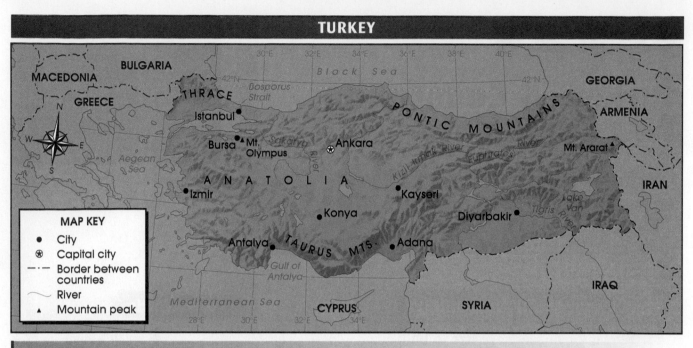

Anatolia is the eastern part of Turkey. Most of Anatolia is covered with a large plateau. What two mountain chains surround the plateau?

Turkey's flag

Mustafa Kemal Ataturk

and plateaus in Asia have a steppe climate. They get some rain and snow. Summers are hot and winters are very cold.

Turkey has two of the important rivers in the Middle East. The Tigris and Euphrates rivers begin in Turkey.

History, People, and Government

People first settled in Turkey thousands of years ago. Later the Ancient Greeks ruled Turkey. Then the Romans ruled Turkey. Greek and Roman ruins can be found in Turkey today.

In 1071 Turks from Asia conquered Turkey. It became a Muslim country. Then in 1453 the Ottoman Turks conquered Turkey. Turkey became part of the large **Ottoman Empire**. The empire fell apart after World War I. Turkey became an independent country in 1922.

In 1923 Mustafa Kemal Ataturk became Turkey's leader. He is called the "Father of Modern Turkey." He changed Turkey into a modern **secular** country. A secular country does not have a religious government. Kemal made the religion of Islam completely separate from the government. All of the people had freedom of religion. Women were allowed to vote. Kemal encouraged people to wear western clothes. All of these changes can be seen in Turkey today.

Today there are about 62 million people in Turkey. The official language is Turkish. About 99 percent of the people in Turkey are Muslims. Small groups of Christians and Jews also live in Turkey. Turkey is the only Muslim country in the Middle East that is a democracy.

About 12 million Kurds live in Turkey. They are the largest minority group in Turkey. The Kurds want their own country. But Turkey does not want the Kurds to rule themselves.

The Turks are proud of their food and culture. People around the world enjoy strong Turkish coffee. **Shish kebab**, small pieces of meat and vegetables on a stick, is a popular Turkish food.

Good storytelling is part of Turkey's culture. Turkish steam baths are also part of the culture. Men and women visit the steam baths at separate times. The baths are places to relax and to talk with friends.

Resources, Cities, and Earning a Living

Turkey has many minerals. It is the only country in the Middle East with large amounts of coal. Turkey also has oil, copper, iron ore, bauxite, and **chromite**. Chromite is a mineral that contains chrome. When mixed with other metals, chrome is used to make car bumpers, door handles, and pans. Turkey has not developed many of its mineral resources.

Coffee seller

A Turkish farming family

This bridge over the Bosporus Strait connects Europe and Asia.

Hagia Sofia

Turkey is a developing country. About half of the people live in cities. Most city people have a higher standard of living than people in villages.

Istanbul is Turkey's largest city and port. It was once called Constantinople. About 10 million people live in and around Istanbul. Part of the city is in Europe. The other part is across the Bosporus Strait in Asia. Two bridges connect the city. Istanbul has many factories. It also has more than 1,000 mosques. One of the most famous places in Istanbul is Hagia Sofia. It was first used as a church. Later it became a mosque. Today Hagia Sofia is a museum.

Ankara is Turkey's capital and second largest city. Many people in Ankara work at service jobs. The city also has many factories.

About 60 percent of the people in Turkey are farmers. Many farmers still use traditional farm methods. Animals are used to do much of the farm work. Still, Turkey grows enough food for its needs.

About 11 percent of the people work at factory jobs. Turkey now earns more money from its factory products than from its farm products. The country also earns billions of dollars from tourism.

Turkey trades with the United States and with countries in Europe and Asia. Turkey imports more products than it exports. So the country has an unfavorable balance of trade.

Looking at the Future

Turkey is working to raise its standard of living. More factories are being built. Most children go to school. Cities have good public transportation.

Turkey also has problems to solve. There are not enough jobs. Many Turks have moved to Germany and other countries in Europe in order to find work. There are not enough schools for children in villages.

Islamic fundamentalism is another problem. Many people do not want Turkey to be a secular country. They want religious leaders to lead Turkey's government. Most Turks want their country to continue to be a secular nation.

Many Turks want stronger ties with Europe. Since 1952 Turkey has been a member of NATO. This organization protects Europe. Turkish soldiers have worked with soldiers from other NATO countries. Now Turkey wants to be a member of the European Union. So far, the European Union has not allowed Turkey to become a member.

Turks are working hard to develop their country. Will their country form closer ties with Muslim countries in the Middle East? Will it become part of the European Union? Today Turkey continues to have ties to both regions.

This young Turkish boy in Anatolia is watching sheep.

Chapter Main Ideas

1. Western Turkey is on the continent of Europe. Eastern Turkey is in Asia.
2. Turkey is a developing country. More than half of the people are farmers.
3. Turkey wants stronger ties to Europe. It belongs to NATO. It wants to join the European Union.

Making telephones in a factory in Turkey

◆ Vocabulary

Find the Meaning   Write the word or words that best complete each sentence on the blank lines.

1. A **strait** is a narrow body of _____ that connects two larger bodies of water.

    land   water   sand

2. **Shish kebab** is a popular type of Turkish _____.

    church   food   steam bath

3. **Chromite** is the _____ from which we get chrome.

    plant   animal   mineral

4. _____ became part of the **Ottoman Empire** in 1453.

    Turkey   Greece   Rome

5. A **secular** government is separated from _____.

    taxes   religion   communism

◆ Read and Remember

Finish the Paragraph   Use the words in dark print to finish the paragraphs below. Write the words you choose on the blank lines.

Mustafa Kemal Ataturk   **Kurds**   **democracy**
Muslim   **women**

Since 1071 Turkey has been a _____ country. In 1923

_____ became the leader of Turkey. He helped Turkey become

a modern country. Laws were changed to allow _____ to vote.

Twelve million _____ are a large minority in Turkey. The

government of Turkey is a _____.

Ankara   European Union   developing   NATO   Istanbul

Turkey is a _____ country where more than half of the people
work as farmers. One part of the city of _____ is in Europe and the
other part is in Asia. The capital is the city of _____. Turkey has
soldiers in the organization called _____. Now Turkey wants to
join the _____.

◆ Think and Apply

Compare and Contrast   Read each phrase below. Decide whether it tells about
Thrace, Anatolia, or all of Turkey. If it tells about either part of Turkey, write the
number of the phrase in the correct part of the Venn diagram. If the phrase tells
about the entire nation, write its number in the center of the diagram.

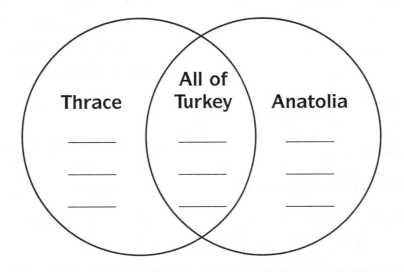

1. steppe climate on plateau and
   mountains
2. Muslim country
3. women vote in elections
4. small region

5. west of Bosporus Strait
6. east of Bosporus Strait
7. earns money from tourism
8. larger part of Turkey
9. fertile hills and plains

◆ Journal Writing

Imagine telling a friend that Turkey is different from other nations in the
Middle East. Write a paragraph in your journal that explains three or more
ways Turkey is different from other nations in the region.

Reviewing a Distance Scale

A **distance scale** compares distances on a map with distances in the real world. We use a distance scale to find the distance between two places. One inch on this map represents 300 miles in Turkey.

Look at the map of Turkey on this page. Use your ruler to measure distances. Then use the distance scale to find the answers. Circle the words that finish each sentence.

1. The distance between Istanbul and Konya is _____.

   ½ inch   1 inch   2 inches

2. The distance between Istanbul and Ankara is about _____ miles.

   50   300   1,000

3. There are about _____ inches between Ankara and Lake Van.

   ¾   1½   2¼

4. The distance between Ankara and Lake Van is about _____ miles.

   200   400   600

5. There are almost 2 inches between Troy and Adana. The distance is almost _____ miles.

   50   75   600

6. By using a ruler and a distance scale, we know the distance from Troy to Lake Van is about _____.

   90 miles   900 miles   2,900 miles

7. By using a ruler and a distance scale, we know the distance between Ankara and Konya is _____ miles.

   10   15   150

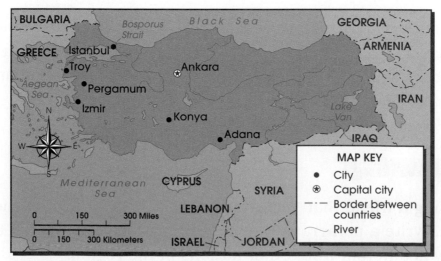

Turkey: Using a Distance Scale

CHAPTER 11

Saudi Arabia: An Oil-Rich Desert Nation

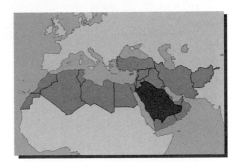

Where Can You Find?

Where can you find sand dunes that are 1,000 feet high?

Think About As You Read

1. What kind of government does Saudi Arabia have?
2. How does Islam affect Saudi Arabia?
3. How have Saudi Arabia's oil resources helped the nation?

New Words

- ◆ sand dunes
- ◆ foreign
- ◆ absolute monarchy
- ◆ modest
- ◆ aba
- ◆ Hajj
- ◆ Kaaba
- ◆ OPEC
- ◆ desalination plants

People and Places

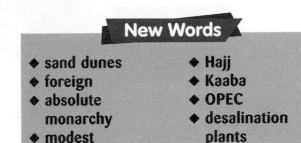

- ◆ Arabian Peninsula
- ◆ Empty Quarter
- ◆ Jidda
- ◆ Mecca
- ◆ Medina
- ◆ King Fahd
- ◆ Great Mosque

Saudi Arabia has more oil deposits than any other nation in the world. It is using the money it earns from selling oil to become a modern, developed country.

Landforms, Climate, and Cities

Saudi Arabia covers most of the Arabian Peninsula. There are also a few other small countries on this peninsula. Find Saudi Arabia on the map on page 84.

Saudi Arabia has mountains in the west near the Red Sea. Some mountains in Saudi Arabia are almost 10,000 feet high. A large plateau covers the central part of the country. In the east, hills and plains cover the land near the Persian Gulf.

Deserts cover most of Saudi Arabia. The country has a very hot desert climate. The country has no lakes and no rivers. A large sand desert is in the south. It is called the Empty Quarter. Some of its **sand dunes** are 1,000 feet high.

The southwest has fertile soil. It is the only region that gets enough rain for farming.

Saudi Arabia covers most of the Arabian peninsula. What three bodies of water surround the peninsula?

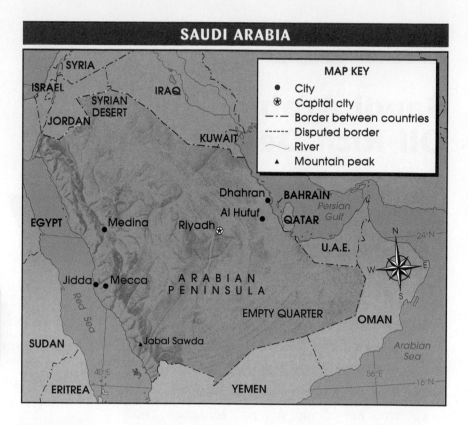

SAUDI ARABIA

MAP KEY
- • City
- ⊛ Capital city
- —·— Border between countries
- ----- Disputed border
- ∼ River
- ▲ Mountain peak

SYRIA
ISRAEL
IRAQ
SYRIAN DESERT
JORDAN
KUWAIT
Dhahran
BAHRAIN
Al Hufuf
QATAR
Persian Gulf
EGYPT
Medina
Riyadh ⊛
U.A.E.
24°N
Jidda
Mecca
ARABIAN PENINSULA
EMPTY QUARTER
OMAN
Red Sea
SUDAN
Jabal Sawda
Arabian Sea
40°E
56°E
16°N
ERITREA
YEMEN

Saudi Arabia's flag

Sand dunes in Saudi Arabia

Most people in Saudi Arabia live in cities. Riyadh, the capital, is near the center of the country. This city has almost 2 million people. It was built at an oasis in the desert. Jidda is a large port city on the Red Sea. Saudi Arabia also has two cities that are holy to Muslims. Mecca is the most important city to Muslims because Muhammad was born there. Medina is the other holy city.

History, People, and Government

Arabs have lived in Saudi Arabia for thousands of years. Many of the people were Bedouins. Bedouins are nomads. They move from one oasis in the desert to another. They travel on camels, live in tents, and raise sheep and goats. Many Bedouins still live in the Saudi deserts today. Some modern Bedouins travel by car instead of on camels.

About the year 570, Muhammad was born in Mecca. He started the religion of Islam. During his life, people living in the Arabian Peninsula became Muslims. Since that time Saudi Arabia has been a Muslim country. More than one billion people in the world today are Muslims.

Today about 19 million people live in Saudi Arabia. The people are called Saudis. Arabic is the official language. One fourth of the people are **foreign** workers, or workers from other countries.

King Fahd is the ruler of Saudi Arabia. He is a member of the royal Saudi family. This family has been important for hundreds of years. Saudi Arabia is not a democracy. It is an **absolute monarchy**. This means the king has full power to make all laws. The king is also the country's religious leader.

Religion and Women

All citizens of Saudi Arabia must be Muslims. They cannot practice any other religion. All Saudi laws are based on Islamic law. There are special police officers who make sure people obey the Islamic laws. Islam allows Saudi men to have four wives. Islam does not allow people to eat pork or drink alcohol. There are no movie theaters, plays, or concerts in the country.

There are strict Islamic laws for women. Girls must study at separate schools from boys. Women are not allowed to drive cars. They cannot ride bicycles. When women leave their homes, they must always be with a male family member. Women cannot work outside of their homes at jobs with men. They can only work with women. Some women work as teachers at schools for

King Fahd

A computer class in Riyadh

Every year Muslim men and women from around the world make a Hajj to the Great Mosque at Mecca.

girls. Other women work as doctors and nurses, but only with female patients.

Islamic laws say women must be **modest**. They must wear clothes that cover their arms and legs. They must cover their hair and faces. So Saudi women have to wear a long black robe called an **aba** when they leave home. An aba covers a woman's head, face, and body.

Muslims believe they must visit the holy city of Mecca at least once during their lives. The visit to Mecca is called a **Hajj**. Muslim men and women from all over the world make this religious trip to Mecca. There they visit the Great Mosque. This huge mosque holds 300,000 people. Inside the Great Mosque is the **Kaaba**, the holiest place in Islam.

Economy and Standard of Living

Oil and natural gas were discovered in Saudi Arabia in the 1930s. One fourth of all the oil in the world is in Saudi Arabia. Most of it is near the Persian Gulf. Saudi Arabia also has other minerals. It has iron, gold, and copper. However, Saudi Arabia has not developed these other natural resources.

Since the 1940s Saudi Arabia has earned billions of dollars from exporting oil. Saudi Arabia is a member of **OPEC**, the Organization of Petroleum Exporting Countries. Saudi Arabia is one of the richest countries in the world. But Saudi Arabia is still a developing country.

Many Saudis worry that some day they will have no more oil to export. Saudis want their economy to

A Saudi woman in an aba

depend less on oil exports. So the country is finding other ways to earn money. It has a favorable balance of trade because it earns so much money from selling oil. It buys cars, food, machines, weapons, and many other products from the United States. But Saudi Arabia is also using its money from oil to build a modern country and to help its people.

About one fourth of the Saudis work at agriculture. The government has built **desalination plants** to take the salt out of ocean water. This water is used to grow food in the desert. Saudi Arabia now grows more than enough wheat. But it must still import more than half of its food.

Saudi Arabia also uses the money from oil to build an economy that is less dependent on selling oil. It is building modern factories and new industries. Today Saudis produce steel, cement, and food products. The country also earns millions of dollars from Muslims from other countries who come to Mecca for the Hajj.

The Saudis are working to raise the country's standard of living. Small villages now have electricity. Cities now have many modern apartment houses. There is free health care for all people. There are free public schools for children everywhere. Still, more than one third of the Saudi people cannot read and write.

Saudi Arabia is working to become a modern, industrial nation. It is already an important nation in the Middle East. It is also a powerful leader in OPEC and the Muslim world.

An oil refinery in Saudi Arabia

Desalination plants like this take the salt out of ocean water.

Chapter Main Ideas

1. Saudi Arabia is a desert country. It has one fourth of the world's oil.
2. All Muslims must visit Mecca on a Hajj. All Saudis must be Muslims.
3. Saudi Arabia is using money from selling oil to become a developed country. It is improving health care and education.

USING WHAT YOU'VE LEARNED

◆ Vocabulary

Finish the Paragraph   Use the words in dark print to finish the paragraph below. Write the words you choose on the correct blank lines.

| Hajj | modest | absolute monarchy | desalination plants |
| aba | Kaaba | sand dunes | |

The Bedouins of Saudi Arabia live in the desert and move from place to place. In the Empty Quarter Desert, there are large hills called _____. The Saudis have built _____ to change ocean water to fresh water. The government of Saudi Arabia is an _____ because the king makes all laws. Saudis believe women must cover their hair, faces, arms, and legs in order to be _____. City women wear a long black robe called an _____. All Muslims try to make a religious trip to Mecca called a _____. The holiest place in Mecca is the _____.

◆ Read and Remember

Complete the Chart   Use facts from chapters 10 and 11 to complete the chart. You can read both chapters again to find facts you do not remember.

Two Countries of the Middle East

	Saudi Arabia	Turkey
What is the official language?		
What is the religion?		
Is there religious freedom?		
What is the type of government?		
What are the resources?		
Is this a developing country?		

◆ Think and Apply

Drawing Conclusions   Read each pair of sentences. Then look in the box for the conclusion you might make. Write the letter of the conclusion on the blank.

1. Saudi Arabia gets almost no rain.
   The country has no lakes or rivers.

   Conclusion: _____

2. All Muslims must try to visit Mecca at least once.
   The holiest places in Islam are in Mecca.

   Conclusion: _____

3. It is against the law in Saudi Arabia to eat pork or drink alcohol.
   It is against the law for women to drive cars in Saudi Arabia.

   Conclusion: _____

4. Saudi Arabia uses money from selling oil to build schools and desalination plants.
   Saudi Arabia uses money from selling oil to bring electricity to small villages.

   Conclusion: _____

5. Saudi Arabia is building new factories.
   Saudi Arabia is earning money from its farm products.

   Conclusion: _____

> **Conclusions**
> **A.** Saudi laws are based on Islamic law.
> **B.** Saudi Arabia is using money from oil to become a developed country.
> **C.** Saudi Arabia wants other ways to earn money besides selling oil.
> **D.** Mecca is a very holy city to Muslims.
> **E.** Most of Saudi Arabia is desert.

◆ Journal Writing

Write a paragraph in your journal that tells how Saudi Arabia is using the money it earns from selling its oil.

Reviewing Bar Graphs

You have learned that a **bar graph** uses bars of different lengths to show facts. This bar graph shows how much oil was produced by five countries in the Middle East in 1995. The amount of oil is measured in barrels.

Study the graph. Then circle the answer for each question.

1. Which country produced the most oil?

Kuwait   Algeria   Saudi Arabia

2. Which country is the second largest oil producer in the Middle East?

Kuwait   Iran   Libya

3. Which countries produced less oil than Iran?

Kuwait and Saudi Arabia

Algeria and Libya

Saudi Arabia and Algeria

4. About how many barrels of oil a day did Saudi Arabia produce in 1995?

2,000   3,000   8,000

5. About how many barrels of oil a day did Libya produce in 1995?

1,000   3,000   4,000

6. Which country produced the least oil?

Algeria   Kuwait   Libya

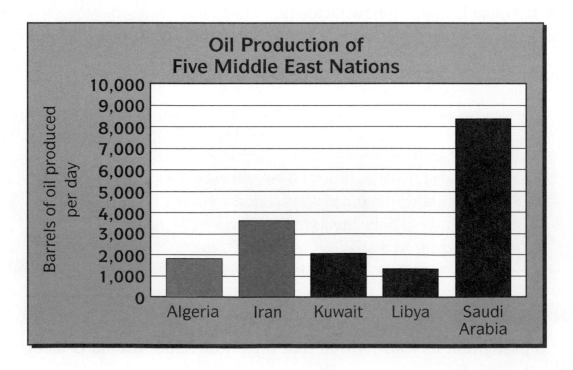

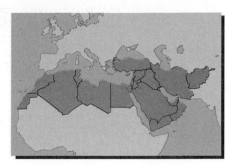

CHAPTER 12

Understanding the Middle East

Where Can You Find?

Where can you find a city that is so crowded that some people must live in a cemetery?

Think About As You Read

1. How are countries solving the problem of scarce water?
2. How has Islamic fundamentalism changed the Middle East?
3. How have wars hurt the Middle East?

New Words

- overpopulation
- cemetery
- aquifers
- conservation
- shah
- missiles

People and Places

- Kuwait
- Syria
- Iraq
- Iran
- Lebanon
- Saddam Hussein
- Queen Noor
- King Hussein

Most of the countries in the region of the Middle East are developing countries. To help their people have better lives, these countries must solve five problems.

Overpopulation, Poverty, and Lack of Water

The first problem in the Middle East and North Africa is **overpopulation**. This means there are too many people living in the region. Many cities are very crowded. Most of the land cannot be farmed. So most countries cannot grow enough food for all their people. Cairo, Egypt, has become so crowded that many poor people now live in a large **cemetery**.

The second problem is poverty. Some countries earn billions of dollars from exporting oil, but most people are poor. Too many people work as subsistence farmers. This region needs more factories and industries.

The third problem is the lack of water in the Middle East. It is the driest region in the world. Some countries, such as Saudi Arabia and Kuwait, have built desalination plants to solve this problem. Saudi Arabia

Many poor people live in this cemetery in Cairo.

A desalination plant

has more of these plants than any other nation in the world. But it is very expensive to change salt water to fresh water. Saudi Arabia and Kuwait use their money from selling oil to pay for the plants. Poor countries do not have enough money for desalination.

Other countries are building dams that save river water in reservoirs. Turkey and Syria have built dams on the Euphrates River. But these dams collect so much water that less river water flows into Iraq. Iraq is angry that it gets less water from the Euphrates.

In Libya water has been found in **aquifers** in the Sahara. An aquifer is an area of underground water. Pipes have been built to carry this water to cities near the coast.

In Israel people use **conservation** to save water. People must use as little water as possible for cooking, bathing, and cleaning. Farmers use drip irrigation to save water. Factory water is sometimes recycled. The government strictly controls the use of water.

Islamic Fundamentalism and War

The fourth problem is the growth of Islamic fundamentalism. One goal of this movement is to win control of governments in the region. The new governments would be based on strict Islamic law. In 1979 Islamic fundamentalists led a revolution in Iran.

The **shah**, or king, of Iran was forced to leave the country. The nation became an Islamic republic. Now everyone in Iran must obey strict religious laws.

Islamic fundamentalists have tried to win control of Egypt. Terrorists from the movement have bombed cities along the Nile River. In 1995 they tried, but failed, to kill Egypt's president. Many people fear that the fundamentalists will continue to spread terrorism.

War is the fifth problem in the Middle East. In Lebanon, fighting between Muslims and Christians led to a long civil war. Large areas of the country were destroyed. Most of the fighting ended in 1991.

Between 1980 and 1988, Iran and Iraq fought a long war. The fighting has ended, but the nations have not signed a peace treaty.

In 1990 soldiers from Iraq took control of Kuwait, Iraq's southern neighbor. Saddam Hussein, Iraq's president, wanted Kuwait's oil fields and its ports on the Persian Gulf. Hussein said Iraq would also attack Saudi Arabia. Iraq refused to leave Kuwait. So in 1991 the United Nations sent soldiers to force Iraq to leave Kuwait. The United States led soldiers from 28 countries in the war to free Kuwait. That war is called the Persian Gulf War. Iraq lost the war, and Kuwait became free again. But Hussein continues to rule Iraq and to make threats against Iraq's neighbors.

Since 1948 the Arab nations have been at war with Israel. Egypt and Jordan are the only Arab countries that have signed peace treaties with Israel. During the Persian Gulf War, Israel did not fight against Iraq. But Iraq fired **missiles**, or weapons with bombs, at Israel. The missiles damaged Israeli cities.

In 1993 the United States helped Israel and the PLO sign a peace agreement. Today the PLO controls part of the land the Palestinians lost in 1948. The two sides do not agree about how much land the PLO should control. But both sides are trying to find a peaceful way to live together in the region.

Most children in the Middle East have better lives than their grandparents had. There are more schools

Many buildings were destroyed during the civil war in Lebanon.

British soldiers in Kuwait in 1991

A new hotel being built in Iraq

and more factories. There is better health care. Some nations are using their money from selling oil to build roads, hospitals, and apartment houses. The people of this region need peace. Then they can work together to solve their problems.

Chapter Main Ideas

1. Overpopulation and poverty are problems in the Middle East. There is not enough farmland to grow food for all the people.
2. Water is scarce. Desalination plants and water conservation are helping the region.
3. There have been many wars in the Middle East. This region needs peace to solve its other problems.

BIOGRAPHY

Queen Noor of Jordan (Born 1951)

Lisa Halaby grew up as a Christian in a rich American family. She studied at Princeton University. In 1978 Halaby married King Hussein of Jordan. She became his fourth wife. She also became a Muslim. Halaby's name became Queen Noor.

The people of Jordan like Queen Noor because she works hard to help their country. She has helped Jordan have better schools. She has helped women and children have better lives. The queen also works with groups that help poor people.

The people of Jordan admire the way Queen Noor has cared for the three children of the king's third wife, Alia. Alia died in an accident. Queen Noor also has four children of her own.

Islamic fundamentalists want Queen Noor to wear traditional Arab clothes. But the queen wears western clothes while she works for Jordan and King Hussein.

Journal Writing
Write a paragraph in your journal about Queen Noor. Tell how her life changed after she married King Hussein.

◆ Vocabulary

Match Up   Finish the sentences in Group A with words from Group B. Write the letter of each correct answer on the blank line.

Group A

1. Underground water is found in _____.

2. Programs for saving water are called _____.

3. The king of Iran was the _____.

4. Weapons with bombs are _____.

5. If there are too many people in a region, there is _____.

Group B

A. missiles

B. shah

C. aquifers

D. overpopulation

E. conservation

◆ Read and Remember

Finish Up   Choose the word or words in dark print that best complete each sentence. Write the word on the correct blank line.

| Nile River | aquifers | Persian Gulf War | Iraq |
| Israel | Iran | United States | |

1. Recycling factory water and using drip irrigation are two examples of water conservation in _____.

2. Libya gets water from underground _____.

3. Islamic fundamentalists have bombed cities near the _____.

4. Iraq and _____ fought an eight-year war over several conflicts.

5. The _____ started after Iraq attacked Kuwait.

6. _____ lost the Persian Gulf War.

7. The _____ helped Israel and the PLO reach a peace agreement.

◆ Think and Apply

Cause and Effect   Match each cause on the left with an effect on the right. Write the letter of the effect on the correct blank line.

Cause

1. Most of the Middle East cannot be farmed,

so _____.

2. Water is scarce in Saudi Arabia and Kuwait,

so _____.

3. Turkey and Syria have dams on the

Euphrates River, so _____.

4. In 1979 Iran became an Islamic republic, so

_____.

5. Egypt has made peace with Israel, so _____.

6. Iraqi soldiers would not leave Kuwait, so

_____.

7. Iraq fired missiles at Israel during the Persian

Gulf War, so _____.

Effect

A. they use desalination plants to make fresh water

B. the United States led soldiers in the Persian Gulf War

C. the shah was forced to leave his country

D. Israeli cities were damaged

E. Iraq is getting less water

F. countries do not grow enough food for their people

G. Islamic fundamentalists commit terrorist acts against both countries

◆ Journal Writing

What are two problems in the Middle East that you think are most important? Write a paragraph that explains the two problems. Then tell how they might be solved.

South and Southeast Asia

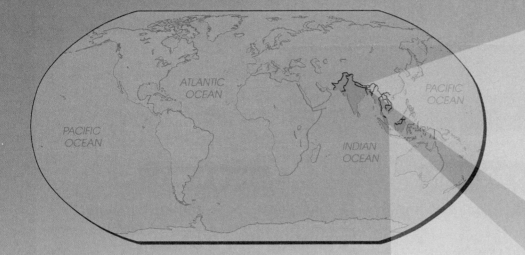

Mount Everest

DID YOU KNOW?

▲ Vietnam is a country with more than 200 rivers.

▲ Singapore is both a city and a nation. It is about the size of Chicago.

▲ Rice has been grown in this region for more than 5,000 years.

▲ The game of chess was first played in India.

▲ The king of Thailand has ruled his country since 1945. No other country in the world today has a monarch who has ruled for so many years.

▲ The tiny country of Brunei is so rich from exporting oil that the people of Brunei do not pay any taxes.

Singapore

WRITE A TRAVELOGUE

Look at the photographs in Unit 3. Then choose two of the countries you would like to visit. In your travelogue, write about what you would like to do in those countries. After reading Unit 3, write two or more paragraphs that describe how South Asia and Southeast Asia are regions.

THEME: REGION

CHAPTER 13

Getting To Know South and Southeast Asia

Where Can You Find?

Where can you find the tallest mountain in the world?

Think About As You Read

1. How do the monsoons help South and Southeast Asia?
2. What kind of land and climate do South and Southeast Asia have?
3. How do most people earn a living?

New Words

- monsoons
- timber
- Hinduism
- Buddhism
- subcontinent
- shifting agriculture
- wet rice farming
- commercial agriculture

People and Places

Himalaya Mountains
- Mount Everest
India
- Indonesia
Brunei
- the Netherlands
- Thailand
- Pakistan
Bangladesh
- Hindus
- Philippines
Deccan Plateau
Indo-Gangetic Plain
Indus River
Ganges River
Vietnam
Mekong River

If you lived in South or Southeast Asia, you might live in a small village. You would probably work on a farm. Rice would be your most important food.

Landforms, Climates, and Resources

The land of South and Southeast Asia is located between the Indian and Pacific oceans. This region has two parts. One part is South Asia. The other part is Southeast Asia. Most of the region is covered with plains and plateaus. The world's tallest mountain chain separates South Asia from the rest of Asia. These tall mountains are the Himalayas. One of these mountains, Mount Everest, is the tallest mountain in the world.

Most of this region is in the tropics. It has a hot climate. **Monsoons**, or seasonal winds, are part of the region's climate. Most of the countries in this region get monsoon winds. From April until October monsoon winds blow in one direction. They bring heavy rain during the summer. Farmers need this rain to grow

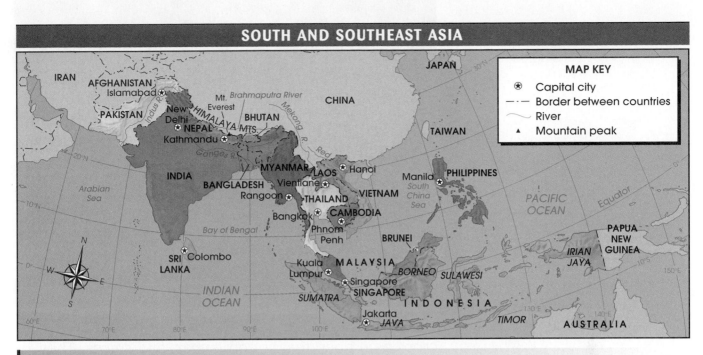

The region of South and Southeast Asia has many islands. The western part of one island belongs to Indonesia. What is the western part of that island called?

food. The winds blow in a different direction for the rest of the year. The winter monsoons bring dry air. There is little or no rain in winter.

South and Southeast Asia have important natural resources. India has coal. Indonesia and Brunei have oil. Some countries get rubber and **timber** from the trees in the region's tropical rain forests. Timber is wood that is used to make buildings and furniture. Countries in the region export some of their resources. But they do not use their resources to make factory goods. Most of the countries in this region are developing nations.

History and People

In the 1500s people from Europe won control of most of the region. For hundreds of years, Britain, France, and the Netherlands ruled many colonies here. Only Thailand, in Southeast Asia, remained free. Now all of the countries in this region are free.

The European countries sent resources from their Asian colonies back to Europe. They used these resources to make factory goods. Europeans also started large plantations to grow cash crops. Today the countries of the region continue to grow such cash

The Himalaya Mountains

A rubber plantation

crops as rubber, tea, cotton, sugar, and spices. They export these crops.

There are many ethnic groups in South and Southeast Asia. The people of this region speak many different languages. They practice different religions. Most people in Pakistan, Bangladesh, and Indonesia are Muslims. Most Indians are Hindus. The religion of **Hinduism** began in India thousands of years ago. The religion of **Buddhism** also began in India long ago. From India it moved to Southeast Asia. People practice Buddhism in many Southeast Asian countries. In the Philippines most people are Christians. There have been many conflicts between people of different religions in this region.

Looking at South Asia

More than one billion people live in South Asia. The area is more crowded than Southeast Asia.

Many of the cities in South Asia are crowded.

South Asia is on a large peninsula. It is called a **subcontinent** because it is a very large piece of land, but it is smaller than a continent. The subcontinent has three parts. One part is the Himalaya Mountains in the north. The second part is the dry Deccan Plateau. There are deserts on the plateau. The Indo-Gangetic Plain is the third part of South Asia. It is south of the Himalayas. This plain surrounds the Indus and Ganges rivers. These rivers start high in the Himalaya Mountains. The land around the rivers is very fertile.

It is densely populated. For thousands of years people have lived in these fertile river valleys.

India is the largest country in South Asia. Pakistan is to the west. Bangladesh is to the east. About three fourths of the people in South Asia live in villages. People live in small huts made of mud. Many villages do not have electricity, running water, cars, or telephones. There are also large cities with millions of people. Most of the people in these cities are very poor. The cities do not have enough jobs for all the people who need work.

Most people in South Asia are subsistence farmers. They work on small farms using traditional methods. As soon as the summer monsoons bring rain, people start planting crops. Rice is the most important crop. India grows almost enough food for its huge population. Pakistan and Bangladesh import large amounts of food.

The Mekong River in Vietnam

Looking at Southeast Asia

Southeast Asia is a crossroads region. For thousands of years people have passed through Southeast Asia as they traveled between Europe, the Middle East, Africa, and Asia. Indonesia, Vietnam, and the Philippines are three of the many countries in Southeast Asia.

Southeast Asia has many islands and peninsulas. It has a long seacoast. Most people live near the sea. There are important rivers in the area. One river, the Mekong, is the fifth longest river in the world.

Southeast Asia has a tropical climate. The monsoons bring summer rains. The hot, wet climate allows tropical rain forests to grow.

Southeast Asia has some very large cities. But most people live in villages. They work at farming.

There are three types of farming in Southeast Asia. The first type is **shifting agriculture**. People chop down trees in the forests and burn them. Then they plant crops. After several years, the soil is no longer fertile. So people move to another part of the forest. There they chop down trees to farm new land. This method destroys the rain forests. It also causes deforestation.

Chopping down trees destroys the rain forests.

Wet rice farming in Indonesia

Picking tea leaves

The second type of farming is **wet rice farming**. Rice seeds are planted in small flooded fields after heavy rains. This work is done by hand. Many farmers are needed. But much of the rice in South and Southeast Asia is grown this way. Rice is the region's main food.

Commercial agriculture is the third type of farming. People grow cash crops on large plantations. Countries export cash crops such as tea and cotton to earn money.

The countries of South and Southeast Asia are working to become more developed. As you read this unit, find out how countries in the region are changing.

Chapter Main Ideas

1. Summer monsoons bring rain to the region. Farmers need this rain to grow food.
2. South and Southeast Asia have huge populations. Most people are subsistence farmers.
3. People have lived in this region for thousands of years. All of the countries except Thailand were once European colonies.

◆ Vocabulary

Forming Word Groups   Read each heading on the chart. Then read each word in the vocabulary list. Form groups by writing each vocabulary word under the correct heading. There is one word you will not use.

Vocabulary List

wet rice farming	commercial agriculture	Buddhism
Hinduism	monsoons	shifting agriculture
subcontinent	timber	

Understanding South and Southeast Asia

Religions	Land and Climate	Types of Farming
1. _____	1. _____	1. _____
2. _____	2. _____	2. _____
		3. _____

◆ Read and Remember

Complete the Geography Organizer   Complete the geography organizer below with information about South and Southeast Asia.

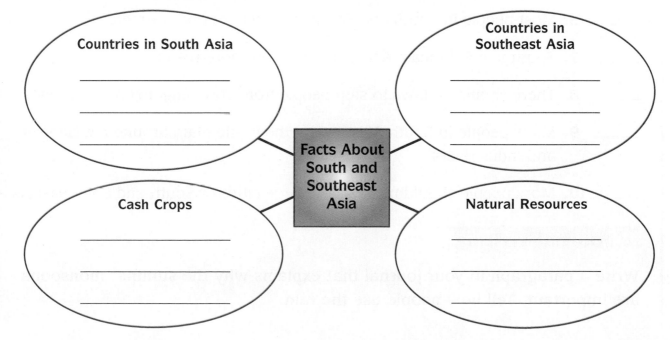

Write the Answer Write one or more sentences to answer each question.

1. How do the monsoons help South and Southeast Asia? _____

_____

2. What did European countries do in this region? _____

_____

3. Which country in Southeast Asia has never been a colony? _____

_____

◆ Think and Apply

Fact or Opinion Write **F** next to each fact. Write **O** next to each opinion. You should find four sentences that are opinions.

_____ **1.** The Indus, Ganges, and Mekong rivers are important to South and Southeast Asia.

_____ **2.** The Himalaya Mountains are the tallest in the world.

_____ **3.** Monsoon winds bring dry air in winter.

_____ **4.** The region needs more plantations.

_____ **5.** European nations began controlling South and Southeast Asia in the 1500s.

_____ **6.** Most people in South and Southeast Asia are poor farmers.

_____ **7.** South and Southeast Asia should export more resources.

_____ **8.** There should be laws to stop people from chopping down rain forests.

_____ **9.** Many people in South Asia live on the fertile plain around the Ganges and Indus rivers.

_____ **10.** More people should move to the large cities of South and Southeast Asia.

◆ Journal Writing

Write a paragraph in your journal that explains why the summer monsoons are important. Tell how people use the rain.

CHAPTER 14

India: Largest Nation of South and Southeast Asia

Where Can You Find?

Where can you find a crowded eastern port city with a modern subway?

Think About As You Read

1. How do problems with the monsoons hurt India?
2. How does the Hindu religion affect Indian life?
3. How is India becoming a more developed nation?

New Words

◆ sacred
◆ Hindi
◆ Sikhism
◆ vegetarians
◆ caste system
◆ caste
◆ untouchables
◆ extended families
◆ jute
◆ religious order
◆ orphanages
◆ orphans

People and Places

◆ Ganges Plain
◆ Brahmaputra River
◆ Sikhs
◆ Mohandas Gandhi
◆ Bombay
◆ Calcutta
◆ New Delhi
◆ Delhi
◆ Taj Mahal
◆ Mother Teresa

India is the largest nation in South and Southeast Asia. It has the second largest population in the world. Almost one billion people live in India. It is a developing nation with big cities and thousands of villages.

India's Landforms, Climate, and Resources

The Himalaya Mountains separate India from China. The Ganges Plain is south of the tall mountains. It is part of the Indo-Gangetic Plain. The Ganges Plain covers northern India. Half of India's people live on this fertile plain. The dry Deccan Plateau is south of the Ganges Plain.

Three rivers flow through the Ganges Plain. They are the Indus River, the Ganges River, and the Brahmaputra River. The Ganges is the longest river. It is **sacred**, or holy, to Hindus. Many Hindus bathe in the holy water of the Ganges River.

Southern India is a large peninsula. It is mostly covered by the Deccan Plateau. There are narrow

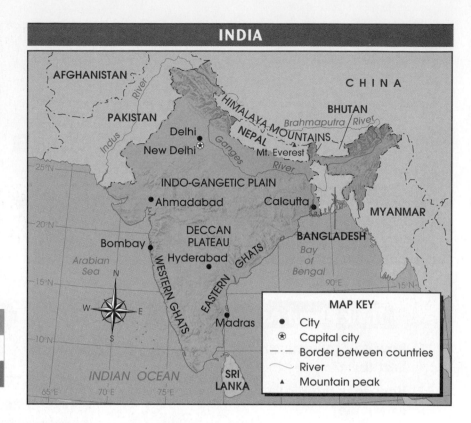

INDIA

India's flag

It is often difficult to cross a river after a monsoon.

plains along the coasts. There are low mountain chains in the east and west near the coastal plains.

India has three climate seasons. One season is cool and dry. Another is hot and dry. The monsoons make June to September a hot and rainy season.

Sometimes the monsoons do not bring enough rain. Then there are droughts. Farmers cannot grow enough food. Sometimes the monsoons bring too much rain. Then the country has dangerous floods.

India has many natural resources. It has coal, iron ore, bauxite, and other minerals. Waterpower from rivers is used to make electricity. India also has some oil. But India imports a lot of the oil that it needs.

People, Religion, and Culture

The people of India are called Indians. They speak 16 main languages. It is hard for people to understand each other because there are so many languages. **Hindi** is the main official language, but only about one third of the people speak it. English is used for government work and business.

Religion is very important to the people of India. Most people believe in the religion of Hinduism. These people are called Hindus. The country also has millions of Muslims. There are also Christians. Other people follow an Indian religion called **Sikhism**. People who follow this religion are Sikhs. All people have religious freedom in India.

Hinduism is a way of life in India. Hindus pray to different gods. They believe it is wrong to hurt people or animals. Cows are sacred to Hindus. There are many cows on city streets. Hindus drink milk from cows, but they do not eat meat from cows. Many Hindus are **vegetarians**, people who do not eat any meat.

The **caste system** is part of Hinduism. A **caste** is a group of people. Each Hindu is born into a caste. People cannot change their caste. Hindu priests and their families are in the highest caste. Farmers are in a lower caste. People of the same caste live near each other in a village. People must marry a person from their own caste.

A Hindu priest

One group of people does not belong to any of the castes. They are called **untouchables**, people who cannot be touched. They have always done the dirtiest jobs. In 1950 the Indian government gave equal rights to the untouchables and to all lower castes.

Religion has caused fighting in India. There have been many fights between Hindus and Muslims. There have also been fights between Hindus and Sikhs.

Family life is an important part of India's culture. Many people live together in **extended families**. This

Cows can often be found on city streets in India.

A boat on the Indus River

means grandparents, aunts, uncles, children, and parents live together. Parents often decide who their children will marry.

History and Government

About 4,500 years ago, people first settled on the fertile land near the Indus River. People later moved into southern India.

In the 1800s Great Britain forced India to become a British colony. The British built railroads, roads, and schools. But the Indians wanted to rule themselves.

After World War I, a great leader named Mohandas Gandhi led India's struggle for independence. Gandhi was against all fighting and violence. He used peaceful protests to force the British to leave India. At last, in 1947 India became an independent country. That same year the eastern and western parts of India became a Muslim nation called Pakistan. Millions of Indian Muslims in India moved to Pakistan. Millions of Hindus in Pakistan moved to India. Today eastern Pakistan is an independent country called Bangladesh.

India is the world's largest democracy. People vote for Parliament members. A prime minister leads the country.

Cities, Villages, and the Economy

Only one fourth of India's people live in cities. About 13 million people live in Bombay. This busy port is the largest city in India.

Mohandas Gandhi

Calcutta is a large port in the east. Calcutta has a modern subway system. It has many kinds of factories. But about one fourth of the people live in slums. Thousands of homeless, starving people live in the streets.

India's capital is in the modern city of New Delhi. An older city called Delhi is next to New Delhi.

One of the most beautiful places in the world is not too far from Delhi. It is the famous Taj Mahal. An Indian emperor had it built in the 1600s to honor his dead wife.

The Taj Mahal

Most Indians live in small villages. There are more than 500,000 villages. Most villages have about 1,000 people. People live in small huts. Most villages do not have electricity or running water. So women must go to the village well to get water for their families. There they learn the latest news from other women. Women carry water in pots on their heads back to their homes. Most village people are poor subsistence farmers. They do not have modern machines or tools. Their main foods are wheat or rice and vegetables.

Indian farmers also grow cash crops on large plantations. India exports cotton, sugar, tea, spices, and **jute**. Jute is used to make rope.

India is becoming an industrial nation. Millions of city people have factory jobs. Today India produces cars, ships, planes, steel, machines, and many other products.

India has a large movie industry. Indians make more than 700 movies each year. The country also earns money from tourism.

A woman carrying water

A Changing Nation

India is working hard to become a developed nation. Illiteracy has been a big problem. About half of the people cannot read. So the government has started many new schools. Most small villages now have an elementary school.

For many years India did not grow enough food. The government has helped farmers learn better ways to grow food. You will read more about this in Chapter 17. Today India grows almost all the food it needs.

India's biggest problem is rapid population growth. To solve this problem, the government gives extra money to families that have only two children.

Indians are building more schools and factories. They are learning better ways to farm. They are solving the problems of their country.

Chapter Main Ideas

1. Hinduism and the caste system are a way of life in India.
2. In 1947 India became free from Great Britain. The government is a democracy.
3. Most Indians live in villages. One fourth of the people live in large cities.

BIOGRAPHY

Mother Teresa (1910–1997)

Mother Teresa grew up in Eastern Europe. There she became a Catholic nun. She was sent to Calcutta, India. Mother Teresa started a **religious order** called the Missionaries of Charity. Other nuns joined the order. They helped Mother Teresa care for starving, dying, sick, and homeless people in Calcutta. Their job was difficult because so many people needed their help.

Mother Teresa started schools and hospitals. She opened **orphanages** to care for **orphans**. She started branches of her organization in many Indian cities. She also started branches in other countries.

In 1979 Mother Teresa won the Nobel Peace Prize. She continued helping India's poorest people. Her health was poor in the last years of her life. She gave her job of running the organization to another nun. Mother Teresa is loved by the Indian people because she helped their country for so many years.

Journal Writing
Write a paragraph in your journal that tells how Mother Teresa has helped India.

◆ Vocabulary

Finish Up Choose the word or words in dark print that best complete each sentence. Write the word or words on the correct blank line.

Sikhism	**untouchables**	**orphanage**	**vegetarians**
Jute	**caste**	**Hindi**	

1. The main official language of India is _____.

2. People who do not eat meat are _____.

3. A Hindu is born into a group called a _____.

4. _____ is a plant that is used for making rope.

5. One of the religions in India is _____.

6. People who do not belong to a caste are _____.

7. A group home for children without parents is an _____.

◆ Read and Remember

Write the Answer Write one or more sentences to answer each question.

1. Where is the Ganges Plain? _____

   _____

2. How do the monsoons help and hurt India? _____

   _____

3. What are India's natural resources? _____

   _____

4. What four main religions do people in India follow? _____

   _____

5. How do people get water in many villages? _____

_____

6. Who led India's struggle for independence after World War I? _____

_____

7. Why was the Taj Mahal built? _____

_____

8. What are the two largest port cities in India? _____

_____

◆ Think and Apply

Finding Relevant Information   Imagine you are telling your friend why India is a developing country. Read each sentence below. Decide which sentences are relevant to what you will say. Put a check (✔) in front of the relevant sentences. You should find six relevant sentences.

_____ **1.** Most people live in small villages.

_____ **2.** Illiteracy is a big problem.

_____ **3.** India exports cotton, spices, tea, and jute.

_____ **4.** Indian factories produce cars, steel, and other products.

_____ **5.** Most people are subsistence farmers.

_____ **6.** Many villages do not have electricity or running water.

_____ **7.** One fourth of Calcutta's people live in slums.

_____ **8.** India grows almost enough food for its population.

_____ **9.** Monsoons bring rain from June to September.

_____ **10.** Farmers use work animals instead of modern farm machines.

◆ Journal Writing

How is life in an Indian village different from the place where you live? Write a paragraph in your journal that tells how the places are different from each other.

A **circle graph** is a circle divided into parts. All the parts form a whole circle. Look at the circle graph on this page. It shows the percent of Indians in each religious group. The graph shows how the total population is divided among five groups of people.

Use the words in dark print to finish the sentences.

Christians   **Muslims**   **Hindus**   **1%**   **Sikhs**   **11%**   **3%**

1. The _____ are 2% of the population.

2. The Muslims are _____ of the population.

3. About _____ of the population is Christian.

4. The graph shows that the _____ are the largest religious group.

5. The _____ are the second largest religious group.

6. The percent of Sikhs plus the group labeled Others is equal to the percent of

_____ .

7. Buddhism began in India. From the graph we can conclude that Buddhists are less

than _____ of the population of India.

Religions in India

Others
1%
Sikh
2%
Christian
3%
Muslim
11%
Hindu
83%

Total Population = 926 million

113

CHAPTER 15

Vietnam: A Changing Country in Southeast Asia

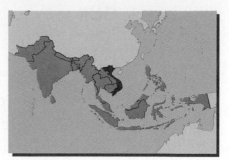

Where Can You Find?

Where can you find a large river delta in southern Vietnam?

Think About As You Read

1. Where do most people in Vietnam live?
2. How has Vietnam changed since 1975?
3. How do people earn a living in Vietnam?

New Words

- ◆ typhoons
- ◆ Tet Festival
- ◆ parallel
- ◆ Viet Cong
- ◆ boat people
- ◆ Communist party
- ◆ average
- ◆ manufacturing
- ◆ textiles
- ◆ investing

People and Places

- ◆ Indochina Peninsula
- ◆ Laos
- ◆ Cambodia
- ◆ Red River
- ◆ Red River delta
- ◆ Mekong River delta
- ◆ Ho Chi Minh City
- ◆ Hanoi
- ◆ Ho Chi Minh
- ◆ Geneva, Switzerland

Vietnam has always been a changing nation. As you read this chapter, think about the ways this Southeast Asian nation has changed during its long history.

Vietnam's Landforms, Climate, and Resources

Vietnam is on the eastern part of the Indochina Peninsula. China is north of Vietnam. Laos and Cambodia are west of Vietnam.

Vietnam's most important rivers are the Red River and the Mekong River. These rivers form two large deltas near the sea. The Red River delta is in the north. The Mekong River delta is in the south. There are coastal plains between the two deltas.

Most of Vietnam is covered with mountains. Forests and jungles cover the mountains.

Vietnam has a tropical climate. Monsoons bring very heavy rains between May and October. These heavy rains sometimes cause dangerous floods on the rivers. The climate is cooler in the mountains.

VIETNAM

Vietnam's flag

Vietnam is located on the Indochina Peninsula. What three countries share borders with Vietnam?

The central part of the coast often has **typhoons**. Typhoons are dangerous tropical Asian storms.

Vietnam has important resources. It has coal, iron, and bauxite. There is oil under the sea near the coasts. The country has not yet developed its resources.

People, Cities, and Culture

About 74 million people live in Vietnam. Most people are Buddhists. Some are Catholics. Vietnamese is the official language.

Most people live on the fertile deltas formed by the Red and Mekong rivers. Only one fifth of the people live in cities.

The largest city is Ho Chi Minh City in the south. It is close to the Mekong River delta. The city has more than 4 million people. It has the most factories and businesses. Hanoi is the nation's capital. It is a port on the Red River.

Families in Vietnam are very close. Members of extended families often live together. Parents and children live with grandparents, aunts and uncles, and cousins.

This family is making rice cakes to celebrate the Tet Festival.

American soldiers in Vietnam
during the Vietnam War

Ho Chi Minh

The Vietnamese people celebrate the **Tet Festival**.
It is the most important holiday. The Tet Festival
celebrates the Vietnamese New Year. It is usually at
the end of January. It is a happy time with parades and
family visits.

History and Government

People first settled Vietnam about 3,500 years ago.
Later, China ruled Vietnam for about 1,000 years.
Vietnam became free in the year 939. It remained a
free country until it became a French colony in the
1800s. The French started plantations that grew tea,
rice, and rubber. They also built cities and railroads.

After World War II, Ho Chi Minh, a Communist
leader in the north, wanted Vietnam to be free and
independent. He led Vietnamese Communists in a war
against France. The French lost the war in 1954. Peace
talks were held in Geneva, Switzerland. During these
talks, Vietnam was divided at the 17th **parallel**, or
line of latitude. North Vietnam became a Communist
country. South Vietnam became non-Communist.

Communists in North Vietnam soon began fighting
to win control of South Vietnam. They were helped by
Communists who lived in South Vietnam. Communists
in South Vietnam were called the **Viet Cong**. Non-
Communists in the south fought against the Viet Cong.
This fight became the Vietnam War.

The United States sent American soldiers to help the South Vietnamese. By 1969 there were more than 500,000 American soldiers in South Vietnam. The war lasted many years. Thousands of people died. In 1973 North and South Vietnam agreed to stop fighting. Both sides signed a ceasefire agreement. The American soldiers returned home.

In 1975 Communists began fighting again for control of all of Vietnam. By April 30, 1975, they controlled the entire country. The north and the south became one Communist country in 1976.

Many non-Communists left Vietnam when the war ended. They often escaped in small boats like this.

At the end of the war, many non-Communists escaped from Vietnam in small boats. They were called **boat people**. These people became refugees in the United States, Australia, and other countries.

Vietnam's **Communist party** now controls the government. All government leaders are from this party. People are not allowed to speak or write against the government.

Standard of Living and Earning a Living

Vietnam has a very low standard of living. Most people are very poor. The **average**, or usual, salary is less than $100 a month. Few people own cars. People often travel on bicycles. People with more money buy motorcycles. Education is important in this developing country. Most people know how to read.

Most Vietnamese people work as subsistence farmers. Rice is a very important crop. Farmers grow rice on the flooded fields of the deltas. Vietnam exports a lot of rice. Since the country has a long coast, fishing is an important industry. There is some **manufacturing**. Some factory products are bicycles, cement, farm tools, and **textiles**. Textiles are different types of cloth.

These girls go to school on bicycles.

During the Vietnam War, tourists did not visit Vietnam. But now tourists are visiting the country again. Vietnam is earning millions of dollars from tourism. Many parts of the country were destroyed during the war. But people are slowly rebuilding their country.

Farmers selling their crops at an outdoor market

Foreign investments are helping Vietnam become more developed.

After the Vietnam War, the Communist government owned all of the businesses. Farms and factories earned little money. The country is changing to a free market economy. People can now own businesses.

For many years, there was no trade between the United States and Vietnam. But now the two nations trade with each other.

Vietnam does not have enough money to develop many new industries and factories. Business owners from Japan, the United States, and other developed countries are **investing** their money to develop Vietnam. They are using their money to start businesses. Business owners hope to earn a lot of money as Vietnam becomes more developed.

Vietnam has changed in many ways during its long history. It is now trying to become a nation with a higher standard of living.

Chapter Main Ideas

1. Most Vietnamese live on the Red River delta in the north and on the Mekong River delta in the south.
2. Vietnam was once ruled by China and later by France. Americans fought in the long Vietnam War.
3. The Communist party rules Vietnam. The country is changing to a free market economy.

◆ Vocabulary

Finish the Paragraph   Use the words in dark print to finish the paragraphs below. Write the words you choose on the correct blank lines.

Communist party   **boat people**   **Tet Festival**
parallel   **Viet Cong**

During the Vietnam War, South Vietnam's government was controlled by people who were against communism, or non-Communists. There were many Communists in South Vietnam who were called the _____. Communists won control of all of Vietnam in 1975. The Vietnamese _____, a political party controlled by Communists, won control of the country. Vietnam was no longer divided at the 17th _____. Many people escaped from Vietnam in small boats. These people were called _____. The Vietnamese usually celebrate the new year at the end of January. This important holiday is called the _____.

average   textiles   manufacturing   investing   typhoons

Today Vietnamese factories are _____ some products such as bicycles, cement, and farm tools. They also manufacture cloth, or _____. Business owners from other countries are _____, or using their money, to start new businesses in Vietnam. Vietnam is a poor country where the usual, or _____, salary is less than $100 a month. Vietman has a tropical climate. Sometimes the central part of Vietnam's coast has _____, or dangerous tropical storms.

◆ Read and Remember

Matching   Each item in Group A tells about an item in Group B. Write the letter of each item in Group B next to the correct answer in Group A.

Group A

_____ **1.** These form two deltas in Vietnam.

_____ **2.** This Communist leader led the fight for independence from France.

_____ **3.** After Vietnam defeated France, peace talks were held in this city.

_____ **4.** This country had more than 500,000 soldiers in Vietnam in 1969.

_____ **5.** This northern city is Vietnam's capital.

_____ **6.** This is the largest city in Vietnam.

_____ **7.** These are two of Vietnam's export crops.

Group B

A. Geneva

B. Hanoi

C. the Red River and the Mekong River

D. rice and rubber

E. Ho Chi Minh

F. Ho Chi Minh City

G. United States

◆ Think and Apply

Sequencing   Write the numbers **1, 2, 3, 4,** and **5** next to these sentences to show the correct order.

_____ Vietnam became a French colony.

_____ China ruled Vietnam for almost 1,000 years.

_____ Vietnam was divided into two countries at the 17th parallel.

_____ American soldiers fought with South Vietnam during the Vietnam War.

_____ Vietnam became a united Communist country.

◆ Journal Writing

Vietnam is a nation that has changed many times. Write a paragraph in your journal that tells three ways that Vietnam has changed during its long history.

Reading a Statistics Table

We use many kinds of statistics, or information given in numbers, to describe a nation's standard of living. The literacy rate tells what part of the population can read. Life expectancy tells the average number of years people live. Average income tells about how much money people earn a year. Most people own telephones when there is a high standard of living.

Population and Standard of Living in Four Countries of South and Southeast Asia

	Average Income	Literacy Rate	Population	Telephones	Men's Life Expectancy
Bangladesh	$1,040	38%	123 million	one for 435 people	56 years
India	$1,360	52%	952 million	one for 112 people	59 years
Vietnam	$1,400	94%	74 million	one for 270 people	65 years
Singapore	$20,000	91%	3 million	one for 2 people	75 years

Study the statistics table. Then use the words and numbers in dark print to finish each sentence. Write the answers on the correct blanks.

Bangladesh	**Singapore**	**life expectancy**	**$20,000**
low	**$1,500**	**Vietnam**	**literacy rate**

1. Vietnam's _____ of 94% is the highest on the table.

2. The lowest literacy rate and average income belong to _____.

3. The average yearly income in Singapore is _____.

4. After Singapore, the highest life expectancy for men is in _____.

5. The average yearly income in three countries is less than _____.

6. The highest standard of living is found in _____.

7. Countries with the highest literacy rate have a higher _____.

8. Developing nations have large populations and _____ standards of living.

CHAPTER 16

Indonesia: One Nation on Thousands of Islands

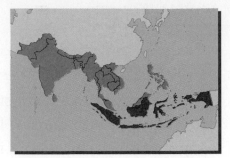

Where Can You Find?
Where can you find the second largest island in the world?

Think About As You Read

1. Why has it been hard for Indonesia to be a united country?
2. What are Indonesia's most important resources?
3. How has Indonesia's standard of living improved since 1968?

New Words

◆ archipelago
◆ ferry boats
◆ volcanic ash
◆ humid
◆ reelected
◆ Bahasa Indonesia
◆ stilts
◆ communicate

People and Places

◆ New Guinea
◆ Irian Jaya
◆ Papua New Guinea
◆ Sumatra
◆ Java
◆ Jakarta
◆ Sukarno
◆ Suharto

If you wanted to visit all of Indonesia, you would have to visit more than 13,670 islands. These islands cover 3,200 miles in the Indian and Pacific oceans. It has been difficult for people who live on so many islands to form a united country.

The Islands of Indonesia

Indonesia is an **archipelago**. An archipelago is a chain of islands. People live on about 6,000 islands in the chain. Six large islands have most of the nation's population. Some of the islands are so small they are not shown on maps. Many islands have no people on them.

The island of New Guinea is in eastern Indonesia. It is the second largest island in the world. Only the western part of New Guinea, Irian Jaya, belongs to Indonesia. The eastern part of the island is a different nation. It is called Papua New Guinea.

INDONESIA

Indonesia is an archipelago of many large and small islands. On which island can you find the capital city of Jakarta?

Sumatra is a large western island. It has important oil resources.

Java is the most important island in Indonesia. It has less than ten percent of the nation's land. But two thirds of the nation's people live on Java. Its soil is very fertile.

Jakarta is the country's capital and largest city. It is in northern Java. This city has about 9 million people. It is a busy port and trade center. It has many factories, banks, schools, and businesses.

It can be difficult to travel around Indonesia. **Ferry boats** help people travel between islands. Airplanes make it faster to travel from island to island. But most people do not have enough money for plane travel.

Landforms, Climate, and Resources

Indonesia has fertile plains near its coasts. Some of these plains have good harbors. There are also beautiful beaches. Mountains, hills, and plateaus cover parts of many islands.

The country has about 60 mountains that are active volcanoes. They can erupt at any time. When they erupt, lava and **volcanic ash** pour out. When this happens,

Indonesia's flag

A volcano on Java

Large parts of Indonesia's rain forests are being chopped down to create farmland.

many people can be killed. Lava and volcanic ash also make the soil fertile for farming.

All of the islands of Indonesia are along the Equator. So the climate is always hot and **humid**.

Indonesia has the world's second largest tropical rain forest. The largest is in Brazil. Indonesians have chopped down large areas of their rain forest. They chop down trees to create new farmland. Trees are also cut down to be made into timber. The timber is exported to countries around the world. Many countries have told Indonesia to stop cutting down the trees. They want Indonesia to save its rain forests.

Indonesia is rich in resources. Oil is the most important resource. Indonesia also produces large amounts of tin and natural gas. The country also has bauxite, copper, gold, and coal.

History of Modern Indonesia

In 1816 Indonesia became a Dutch colony. The Dutch started plantations in the colony. They raised coffee, rubber, and other export crops. The Dutch did not share the money they earned with the island people.

After World War II, many Indonesians wanted their country to be independent. A leader named Sukarno led the fight for freedom. In 1949 Indonesia became a free nation. Sukarno ruled his country as a dictator. While he ruled, the country grew poorer.

Suharto, another leader, became president in 1968. He has been **reelected** five times. He continues to lead the country today.

People and Culture

About 207 million people live in Indonesia. The country has the fourth largest population in the world. The people belong to many ethnic groups. They speak more than 250 different languages. Indonesia has one official language called **Bahasa Indonesia**.

Indonesia is the world's largest Muslim country. Almost 90 percent of Indonesia's people are Muslims. There are many Christians too. There are also some Hindus and Buddhists.

About two thirds of the people live in villages. Most of the houses are built on long poles called **stilts**. The family's farm animals live in the space under the house.

It has been hard for the people of Indonesia to form a united nation. They speak many different languages. They live far apart on thousands of islands. It is hard for people on different islands to **communicate**. It is hard for people on different islands to visit each other. Sometimes mountains and forests separate people who live on the same island. The country is working to be united. All children study Indonesia's official language in school. All people use the same currency. One president unites the country. Islam also joins people together.

The Economy

Indonesia is a developing country. President Suharto has worked hard to improve the economy. Before he became president, millions of people did not have jobs. The country did not grow enough rice for its people. Today most people have jobs. Indonesia now grows so much rice that it exports rice to other countries.

Indonesia earns about one third of its money by exporting oil. The country is a member of the Organization of Petroleum Exporting Countries. OPEC helps decide what the world price of oil should be.

Suharto

Many homes in Indonesia are built on stilts.

Timber is exported from Indonesia to many countries.

A factory in Jakarta

Indonesia has used money from selling oil to develop the country. It has built roads, airports, schools, and factories.

The nation also earns money by exporting other resources. It sells tin, natural gas, timber, and other resources to many countries.

About half of the country's people are farmers. Some people are subsistence farmers. Other farmers work on large plantations. They grow cocoa, coffee, rubber, rice, and spices. Rice and rubber are the most important export crops.

Indonesia has many new industries. Factories make food products, textiles, chemicals, and other goods. But the country still imports most of the factory products it needs.

The people of Indonesia have worked hard to become a united nation. They continue working to improve their standard of living.

Chapter Main Ideas

1. Indonesia is a nation of more than 13,670 islands in the Pacific and Indian oceans. It has a tropical climate.

2. Indonesia has the fourth largest population in the world. It is the world's largest Muslim country.

3. Indonesia earns 30 percent of its money by exporting oil. It is a member of OPEC.

◆ Vocabulary

Match Up   Finish the sentences in Group A with words from Group B. Write the letter of each correct answer on the blank line.

Group A

1. An _____ is a chain of islands.

2. _____ go back and forth between the islands in Indonesia.

3. The dust from an erupting volcano is called

   _____.

4. People share information when they _____.

5. Many village houses are built on long poles

   called _____.

6. A damp climate is _____.

Group B

A. Ferry boats

B. communicate

C. stilts

D. archipelago

E. humid

F. volcanic ash

◆ Read and Remember

Finish Up   Choose a word in dark print that best completes each sentence. Write the word on the correct blank line.

Java   volcanoes   Jakarta   Sumatra   fertile   Equator

1. All of Indonesia is along the _____.

2. Lava and volcanic ash make Indonesia's soil _____.

3. The capital and trading center of Indonesia is _____.

4. An island with large amounts of oil is _____.

5. Indonesia has about 60 active _____.

6. Two thirds of Indonesia's people live on the island of _____.

◆ Think and Apply

Find the Main Idea Read the five sentences below. Choose the main idea and write it in the main idea box. Then find three sentences that support the main idea. Write them in the boxes of the main idea chart. There will be one sentence in the group that you will not use.

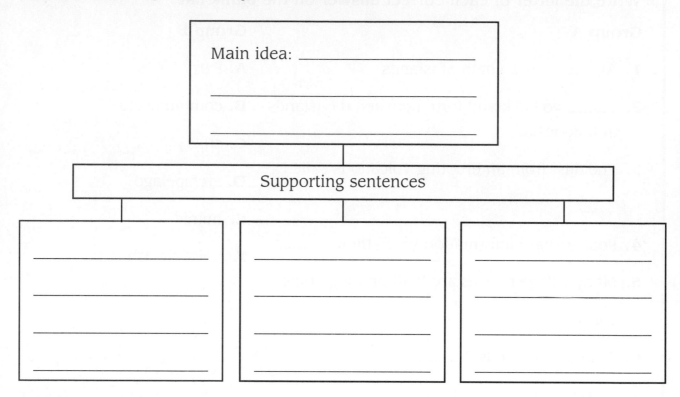

Main idea: _____

_____

_____

Supporting sentences

a. Indonesians speak 250 different languages.

b. It is hard for Indonesia to be a united country.

c. It is too expensive for most people to fly from one island to another.

d. All Indonesians use the same currency.

e. Mountains and forests separate people who live on different parts of the same island.

◆ Journal Writing

Write a paragraph in your journal that tells two ways Indonesia is like other countries of South and Southeast Asia. Then tell about two ways it is different from other countries.

Reading a Time Zone Map

There are 24 time zones on a world map. A **time zone map** shows which parts of Earth are in different time periods. As you travel east, you gain one hour for each time zone that you cross. As you travel west, you lose one hour for each time zone you cross. Indonesia has three time zones. Some time zones curve around islands so that all of the people on an island have the same time. When it is 12:00 noon in Sumatra, it is 1:00 P.M. in Borneo, and 2:00 P.M. in Irian Jaya.

Study the time zone map. Then circle the answer to finish each sentence.

1. If it is 6:00 A.M. in Jakarta, it is

_____ in Borneo.

10:00 P.M.   9:00 P.M.   7:00 A.M.

2. If it is 6:00 A.M. in Sumatra, the time in

Vietnam is _____.

3:00 P.M.   6:00 A.M.   11:00 P.M.

3. If it is 12:00 noon in Borneo, it is 11:00

A.M. in _____.

Java   Sulawesi   Irian Jaya

4. If it is 12:00 noon in Singapore, it is

the same time in _____.

Sumatra   Borneo   Java

5. If it is 2:00 P.M. in Java, it is

_____ in Irian Jaya.

4:00 P.M.   9:00 P.M.   11:00 P.M.

6. Sulawesi will have the same time as

_____.

Sumatra   Timor   Irian Jaya

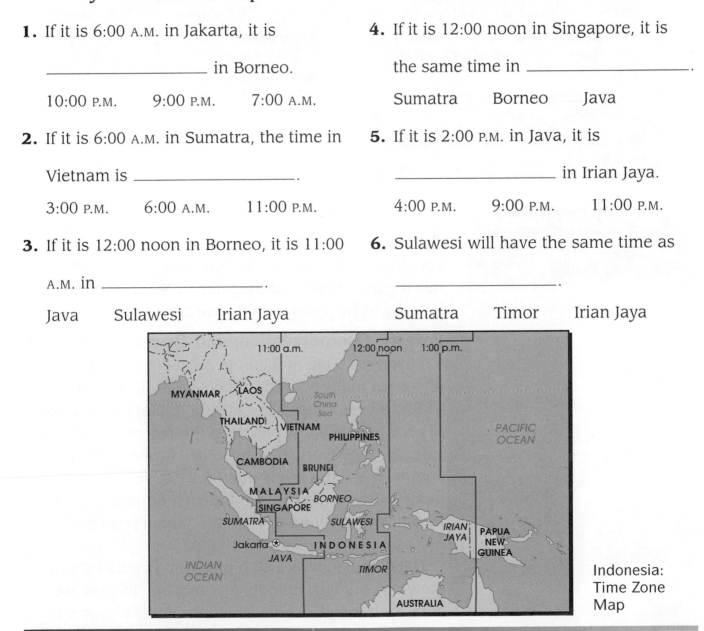

Indonesia: Time Zone Map

CHAPTER 17

Problems Facing South and Southeast Asia

Where Can You Find?
Where can you find a country in Southeast Asia that is a center for world trade?

Think About As You Read

1. How can nations solve the problems of overpopulation and overcrowded cities?
2. How are nations solving the deforestation problem?
3. How has the Green Revolution helped India?

New Words

- sanitation
- Green Revolution
- miracle seeds
- foreign investments

People and Places

- Singapore
- Bangkok, Thailand

The nations of South and Southeast Asia are developing countries. Singapore is the only developed country in this region. These countries must solve five problems in order to help their people live better lives.

Poverty, Overpopulation, and Overcrowded Cities

Poverty is a big problem in most countries of the region. In many countries people earn less than $1,500 a year. Cities like Calcutta, India, have millions of poor people. Most people in the region live in small villages. They work as subsistence farmers. They often do not have extra crops that they can sell to earn money. Governments need to teach farmers modern methods to grow food. Then the farmers can earn more money by selling their crops.

Overpopulation is also a problem. Populations are growing very fast. In India one million children are born each month. The population of this region will

A crowded street in Delhi, India

double in about 40 years. The region will have twice as many people as now. How will its countries have enough food, homes, and jobs for their people?

Governments are trying to solve this problem. They are teaching people to have smaller families. In India, radio and TV programs tell people that it is better to have small families. In Singapore, the government helps families with no more than one or two children.

Overcrowded cities are the third problem. Most of the cities in this region are very crowded. Almost every country has at least one city with more than one million people. Both Calcutta and Bombay have more than 10 million people. Bangkok, Thailand, has more than 6 million people.

Millions of very poor people live in dirty slums that surround the big cities of South and Southeast Asia. But the cities do not provide enough jobs, schools, and services for the people who live there. **Sanitation**, or keeping cities clean, is very difficult in crowded cities. Air and water pollution are also big problems in these crowded cities.

These children live in a slum in Calcutta, India.

Deforestation and War

Deforestation is the region's fourth problem. A large part of the forests in this region have been destroyed. In many place this has caused erosion. Many forests

These trees were planted to replace older trees that have been cut down.

Because of the Green Revolution, India can export some of the rice it grows.

have been chopped down in northern India and in Singapore.

To solve this problem, many nations are planting new trees. These trees replace the ones that have been cut down. Some countries such as Indonesia have passed laws that stop people from exporting timber. The wood cannot be sold to other countries. So fewer trees are cut down.

War is the fifth problem. Millions of people in the region have died in wars. In India and Pakistan, religious groups have fought each other. In 1971 a war began between East and West Pakistan. It began when East Pakistan said it was no longer part of Pakistan. After a nine-month war, East Pakistan became the independent country of Bangladesh.

There have been many years of fighting in Indochina. The long Vietnam War did not end until 1975. There was fighting in Laos and Cambodia. Today most of the fighting in this region has stopped. If peace lasts, nations can work at solving their problems.

How Have Some Nations Solved Problems?

India has worked hard to end its hunger problem. For many years India imported large amounts of rice and wheat. The **Green Revolution** has helped India grow the food it needs. The Green Revolution means farmers use **miracle seeds** and modern methods to grow large crops. Miracle seeds are special seeds that produce larger crops of rice, corn, and wheat. By using miracle seeds, chemical fertilizers, and irrigation, farmers grow much more food. India now exports some of its grain to other countries.

Foreign investments are helping Vietnam, Thailand, Indonesia, and some other countries become more developed. Business owners outside the region use their money to start new industries. These business owners can build new factories. These factories will give people jobs. Singapore now has about 800 businesses that Americans started. These businesses have helped Singapore become a developed country.

Schoolgirls in Thailand waiting in line to play

Tiny Singapore has proved that countries in this region can have a high standard of living. Singapore has become a busy center for world trade.

After many years of war, Vietnam is becoming a better place to live. Children are going to school and learning to read. The literacy rate is high. Tourists are visiting the country and spending money.

The people of South and Southeast Asia want to solve their problems. Then more people will enjoy a higher standard of living.

Chapter Main Ideas

1. The five big problems in this region are poverty, overpopulation, overcrowded cities, deforestation, and war.
2. Foreign investments are helping some nations build new factories.
3. The Green Revolution has helped India grow more food.

An American tourist shows a picture to these Vietnamese children.

Singapore

Singapore is a rich developed country in Southeast Asia. It is a small country with about 3 million people. The country has one main island called Singapore. There are also about 50 very small islands. The capital and only city is in the south of the main island. The capital is the city of Singapore. There are small towns on other parts of the island. Most of the nation's people live in the capital.

Singapore's location is 70 miles from the Equator. So it has a hot, rainy climate. Singapore is near Malaysia and Indonesia. It is on a trade route between Europe, Africa, and Asia. Ships from many nations use the port of Singapore as they travel from one continent to another. Singapore's harbor is one of the world's busiest ports.

Singapore's factories make many kinds of products. They use modern technology. These products are sent to many parts of the world.

At one time many wild animals lived on the island of Singapore. As Singapore built roads and factories, most of the animals were destroyed.

Singapore is a region of very strict government. It is against the law to spit or to cross the street when the traffic light is red. Newspapers cannot write against the government. People are punished when they break the country's strict laws. Most people in Singapore obey the laws.

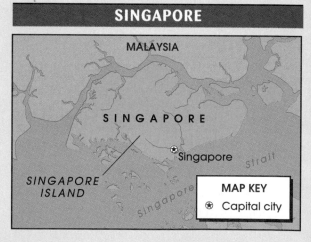

SINGAPORE

MALAYSIA

SINGAPORE

⊛ Singapore

Strait

SINGAPORE ISLAND

Singapore

MAP KEY
⊛ Capital city

Write a sentence to answer each question.

1. Place What kind of place is Singapore?

_____

2. Human/Environment Interaction How did the development of Singapore affect wildlife?

_____

3. Region What kind of region is Singapore?

_____

◆ Vocabulary

Find the Meaning   Choose the word or words that best complete each sentence. Write your answers on the blank lines.

1. A city with poor **sanitation** will be _____.

clean   dirty   modern

2. Singapore has **foreign investments** because people from other nations have

started _____.

businesses and factories   tariffs and taxes   wars and farms

3. The **Green Revolution** helps _____.

lawyers   painters   farmers

4. **Miracle seeds** produce _____.

larger crops   smaller crops   earlier crops

◆ Read and Remember

Complete the Chart   Use facts from the chapter to complete the chart. You can read the chapter again to find facts you do not remember.

Problems of South and Southeast Asia

	What Is the Problem?	How Does the Problem Hurt the Region?	What Is One Way the Problem Is Being Solved?
1.			
2.			
3.			

◆ Think and Apply

Cause and Effect   Match each cause on the left with an effect on the right. Write the letter of the effect on the correct blank.

Cause

1. Overpopulation is a big problem, so
   _____.

2. Many forests have been chopped
   down, so _____.

3. The people of Bangladesh wanted
   to be independent from Pakistan, so
   _____.

4. The Green Revolution helped India,
   so _____.

5. Foreign businesses are starting new
   factories, so _____.

6. Vietnam now has peace, so _____.

Effect

A. they fought a war in 1971

B. tourists are visiting the country again

C. Indian TV and radio programs tell people to have smaller families

D. there is a lot of erosion in the region

E. some countries in the region are becoming more developed.

F. the country now exports rice and wheat

◆ Journal Writing

Write a paragraph about two problems in South and Southeast Asia. Explain what the problems are. Then tell how nations can try to solve them.

East Asia and the Pacific

The Great Wall of China

DID YOU KNOW?

▲ No one has ever been able to count all of the islands in the Pacific Ocean. There may be as many as 30,000 islands.

▲ The world's longest railroad tunnel is in Japan. It connects the islands of Honshu and Hokkaido.

▲ More people speak Chinese than any other language.

▲ China shares its border with 14 nations. No other country has borders that touch as many nations.

▲ There are more sheep than people in Australia and New Zealand.

The Great Barrier Reef

WRITE A TRAVELOGUE

Look at the photographs in Unit 4. Choose one country you would like to visit because it reminds you of the United States. Choose a second country you would like to visit because it looks different from the United States. In your travelogue write about why you want to visit each country. After reading Unit 4, write about three more countries you would like to visit. Tell why each country is a special place.

THEME: PLACE

Looking at East Asia and the Pacific

Think About As You Read

1. What factory products do Americans buy from this region?
2. What are the landforms and climates of East Asia and the Pacific?
3. How do natural disasters hurt this region?

New Words

◆ mainland
◆ temperate zones
◆ inland
◆ natural disasters
◆ tsunamis
◆ free enterprise

People and Places

◆ Oceania
◆ New Zealand
◆ China
◆ Hong Kong
◆ North Korea
◆ South Korea
◆ Taiwan
◆ Hong Kong City
◆ Kowloon
◆ Special Administrative Region of China (S.A.R.)

American stores are filled with many products from the countries of East Asia and the Pacific. There are cameras from Japan and bicycles from Taiwan. There are cotton shirts from China and wool sweaters from Australia. This is a region of trade and industry.

The Region of East Asia and the Pacific

East Asia and the Pacific is a huge region. It has four parts. The Equator divides this region. Three parts are south of the Equator. The first part is Australia. It is a country that is also a continent.

The second part is Oceania. Oceania has the islands of the Pacific Ocean. There are about 25,000 islands in Oceania. New Zealand is the only developed country in Oceania. Oceania and Australia are not crowded. There is room for many more people.

Antarctica is the third part of the region. It is a frozen continent at the South Pole.

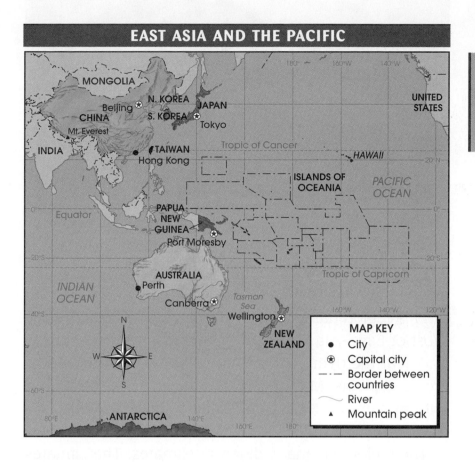

East Asia and the Pacific is a huge region divided by the Equator. What two countries north of the Equator share a peninsula?

The fourth part of this region is north of the Equator. The countries of East Asia cover this part of the region. China, Japan, and Hong Kong are in East Asia. North Korea, South Korea, and Taiwan are also in East Asia. They have most of the region's cities, people, and factories. They are all very crowded. China is the largest country in East Asia. It has more people than any other country in the world.

Hong Kong is a special region in East Asia. It is a busy port and a center of world trade. Hong Kong includes a peninsula off the coast of southeastern China and many small islands. Hong Kong City and Kowloon are its largest cities. Hong Kong was part of China for more than 1,000 years. From the mid-1800s to 1997, the British ruled Hong Kong. Since July 1997, Hong Kong has been ruled by China again. Hong Kong is called the Special Administrative Region of China, or S.A.R. About 6 million people live in this small region.

The busy port of Hong Kong

Landforms and Climate

East Asia includes land on the Asian continent called the **mainland**. East Asia also includes the

An island in the Pacific

island countries of Japan and Taiwan. These islands are near the mainland.

This region has many landforms. Mountains cover most of East Asia. There are plains near the coasts and near the rivers. Most East Asians live on these crowded plains. Many islands in the Pacific are covered with mountains. Most of Australia is covered with plains and plateaus.

The region has many different climates. The climates to the north and south of the tropics are called the **temperate zones**. The climate in these zones is not too hot or too cold. Japan, Korea, and most of China are in the northern temperate zone. New Zealand and southern Australia are in the temperate zone south of the Equator.

Monsoons bring summer rains to the coasts of East Asia. **Inland** areas, or places that are far from the ocean, are drier. Parts of western China have a desert climate. Most of East Asia has cold, dry winters.

Most of the islands of Oceania have a warm climate. New Zealand and some other islands get a lot of rain. Other islands get only a few inches of rain a year. Northern Australia has a warm, dry climate. The climate in southern Australia is cooler and rainier.

Natural Disasters

Natural disasters are terrible accidents caused by nature. Many natural disasters happen in East Asia and the Pacific. Japan, Taiwan, and many Pacific islands have volcanoes that sometimes erupt. Erupting volcanoes destroy homes and sometimes kill people.

Winter in northern Japan

This part of the world also has many earthquakes. In an earthquake the ground shakes and the land cracks. Earthquakes destroy homes, buildings, and bridges. Many people have been killed during strong earthquakes. This region has more earthquakes and volcanoes than any other part of the world.

Typhoons also destroy homes, farms, and buildings in this region. These dangerous tropical storms bring high winds and heavy rains.

Tsunamis are huge, dangerous waves. They are caused by underwater earthquakes. They crash into the coasts of East Asia and the Pacific Islands.

An earthquake destroyed these buildings in Japan.

Governments and Economies

There are different kinds of governments in East Asia and the Pacific. Australia, New Zealand, and Japan are democracies. China and North Korea have Communist governments. Dictators lead these governments. The people have little freedom.

China and North Korea have command economies. In a command economy, the government owns all of the farms, factories, and businesses. The government decides salaries and prices. In the 1980s China's government began to allow some **free enterprise**.

Japan, South Korea, and Hong Kong have free market economies. People can own and control their own businesses. They decide salaries and prices. This is also called free enterprise. But now China may have more control over Hong Kong's businesses.

Japan, South Korea, Hong Kong, and Taiwan have many factories and industries. They have strong economies. They manufacture cameras, computers, cars, and hundreds of other products. They are important centers for trade. They earn billions of dollars by exporting their products to all parts of the world. Their people enjoy a high standard of living. Australia and New Zealand also have high standards of living.

Tsunamis cause damage to islands in the Pacific.

China is still a developing nation. Most of the people are farmers. But the country now has many kinds of factories. China exports factory products to all parts of the world.

The countries of East Asia are all very crowded. Which country has the most cities with more than 2 million people?

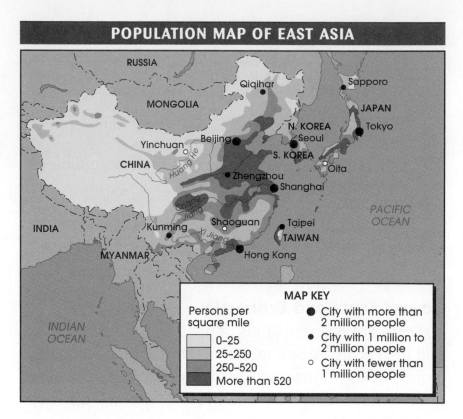

POPULATION MAP OF EAST ASIA

RUSSIA

Qiqihar

Sapporo

MONGOLIA

JAPAN

N. KOREA

Tokyo

Yinchuan

Beijing

Seoul

S. KOREA

CHINA

Huang He

Oita

Zhengzhou

Shanghai

Chang Jiang

PACIFIC OCEAN

INDIA

Kunming

Shaoguan

Taipei

Yi Jiang

TAIWAN

MYANMAR

Hong Kong

INDIAN OCEAN

MAP KEY

Persons per square mile

- 0–25
- 25–250
- 250–520
- More than 520

● City with more than 2 million people

● City with 1 million to 2 million people

○ City with fewer than 1 million people

A Buddhist shrine in Japan

A Region of Many Cultures

The people of this region belong to many ethnic groups. They speak many different languages.

Most people in Australia and New Zealand are Christians. Buddhism is an important religion in East Asia. Communist leaders in China and North Korea discourage people from practicing any religion.

More people live in East Asia and the Pacific than in any other part of the world. Americans use products from this region every day. As you read Unit 4, find out why this region is important in today's world.

Chapter Main Ideas

1. East Asia has crowded countries. Most of the people live on plains near the coasts and rivers. Australia and the Pacific Islands are not crowded.
2. Japan, South Korea, Hong Kong, and Taiwan have many industries. They export products to many countries.
3. China has more than one billion people. Its Communist government now allows people to own businesses and factories.

◆ Vocabulary

Analogies   Use the words in dark print that best complete the sentences.

tsunami   temperate zones   free enterprise
inland   natural disaster   mainland

1. Japan is to island as China is to _____.

2. Hot climate is to tropics as mild climate is to _____.

3. Coastal is to near the coast as _____ is to away from the coast.

4. Deforestation is to a problem made by people as earthquake is to a

_____.

5. Typhoon is to storm as _____ is to wave.

6. Communism is to command economy as _____ is to free market economy.

◆ Read and Remember

Finish Up   Choose the word or words in dark print that best complete each sentence. Write the word or words on the correct blank line.

temperate zones   East Asia   Communist
summer   Oceania   dictators

1. There are about 25,000 Pacific islands in an area called _____.

2. Most of this region's people, factories, and cities are in _____.

3. Japan and New Zealand are in the _____ because they are north and south of the tropics.

4. Monsoons bring _____ rain to the coast of East Asia.

5. Some countries in this region are ruled by leaders called _____.

6. China and North Korea have _____ governments.

Write the Answer   Write one or more sentences to answer each question.

1. What products are made in East Asia? _____

_____

2. What countries are in the temperate zone? _____

_____

3. What are the developed countries of this region? _____

_____

◆ Think and Apply

Categories   Find the best title for each group from the words in dark print. Write the title on the line above each group.

High Standard of Living   **The Pacific Region**   **Australia**
Natural Disasters   **East Asia**   **China**

1. _____

Antarctica
Australia
Oceania

2. _____

Taiwan and Hong Kong
North and South Korea
China and Japan

3. _____

typhoons
earthquakes and volcanoes
tsunamis

4. _____

Australia and New Zealand
Japan and South Korea
Hong Kong and Taiwan

5. _____

more than one billion people
Communist government
allows some free enterprise

6. _____

a continent and a country
plains and plateaus
democracy

◆ Journal Writing

Look at the car, television, radio, camera, or other products your family or someone you know may own. Which products are from East Asia and the Pacific? Write a paragraph in your journal that tells where many of these products were produced.

CHAPTER 19

China: Asia's Largest Nation

Think About As You Read

1. What happened at Tiananmen Square?
2. How did Deng Xiaoping help China's economy?
3. How has the standard of living in China improved?

New Words

- protest
- demonstrations
- collectives
- contracts
- profits
- dikes
- characters
- herbs
- acupuncture

People and Places

- Huang He (Yellow River)
- the Great Wall of China
- Tiananmen Square
- Beijing
- Deng Xiaoping
- Xi Jiang (West River)
- Chang Jiang (Yangtze River)
- Shanghai
- Confucius

More than one billion people live in China. It has more people than any other country in the world. It is only a little larger than the United States. But China struggles to feed four times more people than the United States.

History, Government, and Protests at Tiananmen Square

China is a very old country. Thousands of years ago, people settled on fertile plains around the Huang He River. Later they settled in other parts of China.

More than 2,000 years ago, the Chinese began building the Great Wall of China. They built the wall across northern China. It was built to stop enemies from attacking China. When it was finished, the wall was more than 1,500 miles long. Many tourists still visit the Great Wall each year.

For thousands of years, most Chinese were hungry and poor. Many people believed communism would solve China's problems. In the early 1900s, Chinese

China has many kinds of landforms. What mountain chain is located in the southwestern part of China?

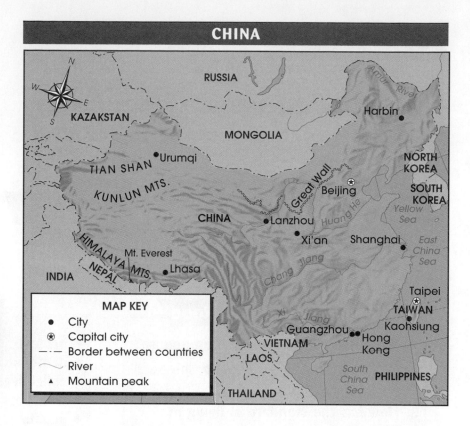

CHINA

MAP KEY
- City
- ⊛ Capital city
- -·- Border between countries
- ~ River
- ▲ Mountain peak

China's flag

Student protestors at Tiananmen Square

Communists began fighting to control the government. Since 1949 Communists have ruled China.

China's non-Communist leaders fled China in 1949. They escaped to the nearby island of Taiwan. In Taiwan they started a non-Communist government. Today Taiwan is a developed country with many industries. Taiwan has a much higher standard of living than China.

The Chinese Communist party has ruled China's government since 1949. People have little freedom. There is no freedom of speech. People cannot **protest** against the government.

In 1989 Chinese students held **demonstrations** in Tiananmen Square to show they wanted more freedom. This happened in the capital, Beijing. China's leader, Deng Xiaoping, sent Chinese soldiers to attack the protesting students. Many students were killed. There is still little freedom in China today.

Economy and Standard of Living

China has a command economy. For many years the government owned all farms, factories, and businesses. But China still had millions of hungry people.

In the 1980s Deng Xiaoping began to improve the economy. He allowed foreign countries to invest their money in Chinese factories. He allowed trade with many countries. Deng bought new machines and technology from other countries. He started new factories in villages. Deng allowed people to own their own small restaurants and businesses.

Deng Xiaoping wanted farmers to grow more food. He knew farmers were not happy working on the huge government-owned farms called **collectives**.

Deng decided that the government would give **contracts** to all farmers. These contracts told farmers how much to grow and how much to sell to the government. Farmers could keep all extra crops for themselves. They could sell these crops and keep the **profits**. So the farmers worked harder to grow much more food. China now has enough food for its huge population. It exports rice to other countries.

China is still a poor country. But most Chinese enjoy a higher standard of living today than they did before 1949. Most children now go to school. Most people receive medical care. Most people now own a bicycle, a radio, and a sewing machine. The standard of living is a little higher in cities. But people who live in the cities live in tiny apartments. Few people in China own cars. Most people travel on bicycles. There are more than 200 million bicycles in China.

These men own their own grocery store in northern China.

A Chinese village

Mountains and deserts cover much of western China.

A ship on the Chang Jiang

China's Landforms, Climate, and Resources

China has many kinds of landforms and climates. Less than 15 percent of all Chinese land can be farmed. Much of China's land in the west is covered with mountains and plateaus. Only a small part of the population lives there. The tall Himalaya Mountains are in the southwest. Large deserts also cover part of the west. Western China has a cold, dry climate.

Most of the country's cities, farms, and people are in eastern China. The east has a long coast. Plains, hills, and low mountains cover the east. People live on fertile plains near the coast and the rivers.

Eastern China has three long rivers. These rivers are surrounded by fertile plains. The Huang He (Yellow River) is in the north. The Xi Jiang (West River) is in southern China. China's longest river is the Chang Jiang (Yangtze River). It is the third longest river in the world. Ships travel on the Chang Jiang for hundreds of miles.

The Huang He has had many floods. These floods have destroyed farms and villages. But silt in the flood waters has made the river valley fertile. To control the floods, the Chinese have built dams and **dikes**, or special walls, on the river.

Monsoons bring rain to eastern China in the summer. The southeast is warmer and wetter than other parts of China. The Chinese grow rice there. The climate is cooler in the north. So northern farmers grow wheat instead of rice.

China has many natural resources. It has oil, coal, and iron. It uses waterpower from its rivers to make electricity. China has gold, silver, and tin. Uranium and bauxite are other important minerals.

Cities, Language, and Culture

Today about one fourth of China's people live in cities. There are 30 cities that have more than one million people. Shanghai is China's largest city. It has more than 12 million people. It is an important port. It has many factories. Beijing is China's capital. It is near iron and coal mines. This city has large steel factories.

Shanghai

The Chinese language does not have an alphabet. Instead the Chinese write with little pictures called **characters**. Each character shows a word or an idea. To read a Chinese newspaper, a person must know at least 3,000 characters.

The Chinese have followed the teachings of their great teacher Confucius for more than 2,500 years. Confucius taught people to respect parents, teachers, and government leaders. He also said people must be honest and kind.

For thousands of years, the Chinese have made medicines from plants called **herbs**. They also invented a system called **acupuncture**. Acupuncture doctors push small needles into different parts of the body. These needles treat disease and stop pain.

Looking at the Future

China's leaders believe the country will not have enough food if its population continues to grow. So China's laws now allow couples to have only one child. Some couples are allowed to have two children. Couples are punished if they have more children.

In July 1997 China began to rule the small region of Hong Kong. Hong Kong had been ruled by Great Britain since the mid-1800s. Hong Kong has a much higher standard of living than China.

China's Communist leaders want Hong Kong to remain a rich industrial region. They want Hong Kong to share the money it earns with China. So most

A statue of Confucius

Making medicine from herbs

people believe Hong Kong will continue to have a free market economy. But the people of Hong Kong may have less freedom. No one knows how China's Communist government will change Hong Kong.

The world is watching China. Can China continue to grow enough food for its huge population? Will people be allowed to enjoy more freedom? China will always be an important country.

Chapter Main Ideas

1. Most of China's people live in the east. There are fertile plains near the coast and around three long rivers.

2. Since 1949 China has been a Communist country. The people have little freedom.

3. Deng Xiaoping improved China's economy. Farmers grow much more food. There is more industry.

BIOGRAPHY

Deng Xiaoping (1904–1997)

Deng Xiaoping became China's powerful leader in 1977. At the time he was 72 years old. China was a very poor country.

Deng decided that free enterprise would help China's economy. Most Communists were against free enterprise. But Deng wanted to help China's economy. He allowed farmers and business owners to make profits. Many new factories were started. Deng allowed foreign countries to start factories in China. He allowed the United States and other countries to have more trade with China. China's economy grew stronger.

Deng did not believe in democracy. He sent the Chinese Army to attack the student protesters at Tiananmen Square.

Deng died when he was 92 years old. He had helped China become a more modern nation.

Journal Writing
Write a paragraph in your journal that tells how Deng Xiaoping helped and hurt China.

◆ Vocabulary

Finish Up Choose the word in dark print that best completes each sentence. Write the word on the correct blank line.

collectives	**contracts**	**demonstrations**	**dikes**
profits	**protest**	**characters**	

1. The symbols that are used in Chinese writing are called _____.

2. Walls that are built to stop rivers from flooding are _____.

3. Huge farms that are owned by the government are called _____.

4. When you speak out against the government, you _____.

5. Large meetings of people who want changes are _____.

6. The money people earn from selling their products is called _____.

7. Written agreements between a person and the government or between two or more people are called _____.

◆ Read and Remember

Write the Answer Write one or more sentences to answer each question.

1. Where did the early Chinese people settle? _____

    _____

2. What happened in China in 1949? _____

    _____

3. What kind of government does Taiwan have? _____

    _____

4. What happened at Tiananmen Square in 1989? _____

    _____

5. How do most Chinese travel? _____

_____

6. How many children does the government allow a couple to have?

_____

7. What are China's three long rivers? _____

_____

8. Where do most of China's people live? _____

_____

9. What is China's capital city? _____

_____

10. What happened in July 1997? _____

_____

◆ Think and Apply

Sequencing   Write the numbers **1, 2, 3, 4,** and **5** next to these sentences to show the correct order.

_____ Non-Communists escaped to the island of Taiwan.

_____ Chinese Communists fought to win control of the government.

_____ Deng Xiaoping sent soldiers to attack protesting students at Tiananmen Square.

_____ China took control of Hong Kong.

_____ China became a Communist country.

◆ Journal Writing

The laws of China allow most couples to have only one child. Write a paragraph in your journal that tells why China has this law. Tell whether you think the law will help China.

Reviewing Latitude and Longitude

Every place on Earth has its own latitude and longitude. Shanghai, China, has a latitude of 31°N and a longitude of 121°E. We say that the latitude and longitude of Shanghai is 31°N, 121°E.

Look at the map of China below. Then finish each sentence in Group A with an answer from Group B. Write the letter of the correct answer on the blank line.

Group A

1. The latitude of Beijing is ——.

2. The longitude of Guangzhou is ——.

3. The city of Urumqi has a latitude and longitude of ——.

4. The city of —— has a latitude and longitude of 29°N, 91°E.

5. The city of —— has a latitude and longitude of 46°N, 127°E.

Group B

A. 40°N

B. 113°E

C. Lhasa

D. Harbin

E. 44°N, 87°E

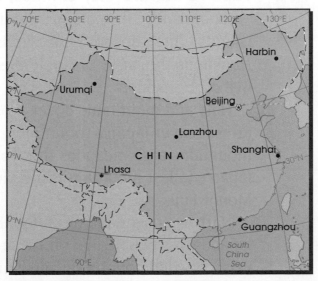

China: Latitude and Longitude

CHAPTER 20

Japan: Asia's Industrial Leader

Where Can You Find?
Where can you find the palace of the emperor?

Think About As You Read

1. Why is Japan a crowded country?
2. What kinds of industries are in Japan?
3. Why does Japan have a favorable balance of trade?

New Words

- Shinto
- kimonos
- bonsai
- robots
- terraces
- dormant

People and Places

- Honshu
- Mount Fuji
- Kobe
- Sea of Japan
- Tokyo
- Sapporo
- Hokkaido

Japan is a crowded country with few natural resources. There is little farmland. Most people would expect Japan to be a poor country. But Japan is the richest country in Asia. It is Asia's industrial leader.

Japan's Landforms, Climate, and Resources

Japan is an archipelago country. It has four large islands. There are also thousands of small islands. Honshu is the largest island. Most Japanese people live on Honshu.

Hills and mountains cover most of Japan. Thick forests cover Japan's mountains. About 60 of the mountains are volcanoes that sometimes erupt. Japan's tallest mountain is a beautiful volcano called Mount Fuji.

Narrow coastal plains cover about one fifth of Japan. Most people live on these plains. Japan is a very crowded country because many people live on this small amount of land.

Japan has more earthquakes than any other nation. It has more than 1,000 earthquakes each year. Most of

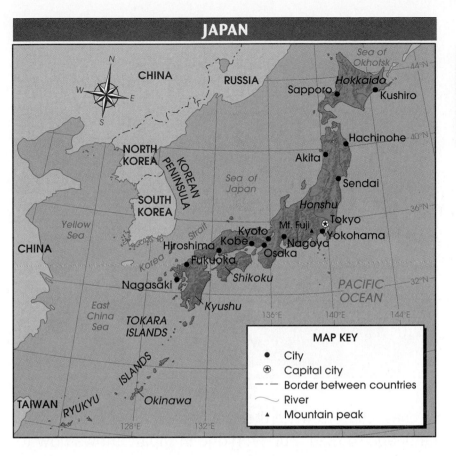

JAPAN

CHINA
RUSSIA
Sea of Okhotsk
Hokkaidō
Sapporo
Kushiro
NORTH KOREA
KOREAN PENINSULA
Hachinohe
Akita
SOUTH KOREA
Sea of Japan
Sendai
Yellow Sea
Honshu
Mt. Fuji
Tokyo
CHINA
Kyoto
Yokohama
Korea Strait
Kobe
Nagoya
Hiroshima
Osaka
Fukuoka
Shikoku
Nagasaki
PACIFIC OCEAN
Kyushu
East China Sea
TOKARA ISLANDS
TAIWAN
RYUKYU
ISLANDS
Okinawa

MAP KEY
- City
- ⊛ Capital city
- – · – Border between countries
- River
- ▲ Mountain peak

Japan is an archipelago country with four large islands and many small ones. What is the name of Japan's largest island?

Japan's flag

them are so small that no one feels them. But some cause great damage. In 1995 an earthquake in the city of Kobe killed more than 5,000 people.

The seas are important to Japan. The Sea of Japan is to the west of Japan. The Pacific Ocean is to the east. No place in the country is more than 100 miles from the sea. The Japanese use the seas for shipping and trading. Fishing is an important industry. The Japanese eat a lot of fish.

Japan's climate changes as you move from south to north. Islands in the south have hot summers and mild winters. The northern islands have cold winters and cool summers. But the island of Honshu has warm, humid summers and cold winters.

Mount Fuji is a beautiful volcano.

Japan has few resources. It gets wood from its forests. It creates some hydroelectric power from its rivers. Japan must import coal, oil, and raw materials.

People, Culture, and Government

About 126 million people live in Japan. They speak the Japanese language. They use thousands

155

This man grows bonsai trees.

A Shinto shrine

of characters to write their language. It is a difficult language to read. But everyone in Japan knows how to read and write. The Japanese people spend many years in school.

Many people in Japan practice both the **Shinto** and Buddhist religions. People who believe in the Shinto religion pray to many gods. These gods are found in rivers, mountains, trees, and other forms of nature. The country has thousands of Shinto and Buddhist temples.

Japan is a very modern country, but the Japanese people love their old traditions. People bow to each other to say hello and goodbye. They show great respect for parents and for older people. They remove their shoes before they enter a home. They cover the floors of their homes with straw mats. People sometimes wear beautiful robes called **kimonos**. Some people enjoy planting small beautiful gardens. They grow tiny trees called **bonsai** trees in flower pots.

The government of Japan is a democracy and a constitutional monarchy. It has a parliament and a prime minister. It also has an emperor. The emperor has no power in the government.

Japan: An Industrial Giant

Japan has a strong economy. Japan makes more factory products than all of the nations in Western Europe. In some years Japan produces more cars than the United States. The Japanese make excellent televisions, cars, cameras, computers, and other products. Their factories have the newest technology. Factories often use machines called **robots** to do many jobs.

Trade has helped Japan become a rich country. Japan imports raw materials for its factories. It exports huge amounts of factory products. Japan limits the number of products it buys from the United States and other countries. So Japan has a favorable balance of trade. It exports much more than it imports.

About one third of the Japanese people work for large companies. These companies make their workers feel like they are part of a large family. They treat their workers well. People work hard and receive good salaries. Many people work for one company until they are ready to retire.

Robots do many jobs in Japan. This robot is repairing power lines.

Farms, Cities, and Standard of Living

Japan has many mountains, so there is little farmland and most farms are small. Only a small part of the population works at farming. The Japanese are excellent farmers. They build **terraces** into the sides of hills so

The Japanese grow rice on terraces built into the sides of hills.

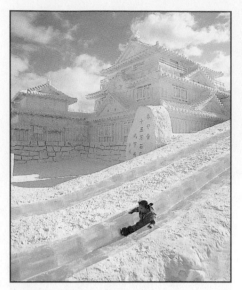
Sapporo's ice festival

they can grow more crops. Terraces are large, flat areas of land for planting crops. The Japanese use fertilizers, good seeds, and modern machines. Farmers grow about two thirds of the food the country needs. Rice is the most important crop. Japan must import some of its food.

About three fourths of Japan's people live in cities. Most big cities are on the coast of the island of Honshu. Tokyo is Japan's capital and largest city. It is also a busy port. Tokyo is one of the largest cities in the world. It is also one of the most crowded. Most people travel around Tokyo by subway. Special city workers push people into the crowded trains so the doors will close. Tokyo is Japan's main business and arts center. It is also the home of the emperor's palace. People are allowed to visit the gardens around this famous palace.

Sapporo is the only large city on the northern island of Hokkaido. Every winter people visit Sapporo's ice festival. Visitors see temples, buildings, and statues that are carved out of ice. People can travel from Tokyo to Sapporo in very fast bullet trains. These trains go through a long tunnel that connects the islands of Honshu and Hokkaido.

Most people in Japan are part of the middle class. They have a good life. But Japan has two big problems. It is too crowded. There is a lot of pollution. Cars and factories are making the air and water dirty.

Look around your home. Look at the cars in the street. You will see many products from Japan. Japan is Asia's industrial leader.

City workers helping people into a Tokyo subway

Chapter Main Ideas

1. Japan has few natural resources. It uses imported raw materials in its factories.
2. Most of Japan is covered with mountains. Most people live on narrow coastal plains.
3. Japan is the richest country in Asia. It imports large amounts of factory products. Most people belong to the middle class.

The Ring of Fire

The Ring of Fire is a chain of volcanoes that surrounds the Pacific Ocean. Alaska, Hawaii, California, and western South America are in the eastern part of the Ring of Fire. Japan, New Zealand, Indonesia, and other Pacific islands are in the western part. Countries in the Ring of Fire have more earthquakes and volcanoes than countries in other regions.

Volcanoes and earthquakes occur because of changes that take place deep inside the earth. Earth is covered with 30 large, rocky sheets called plates. These plates are under the oceans and continents. Sometimes the plates crash into each other. Sometimes the plates pull apart. These movements cause earthquakes and volcanoes.

Scientists never know when a volcano will erupt. Beautiful Mount Fuji erupted in 1707. Since then it has been **dormant**, or quiet. It is possible Mount Fuji will one day erupt again.

A terrible earthquake destroyed part of Tokyo in 1923. More than 100,000 people died. The Japanese rebuilt their city. But they know it can be destroyed again by another earthquake. Millions of people who live in the Ring of Fire know there can be another natural disaster at any time.

THE RING OF FIRE

ASIA

NORTH AMERICA

PACIFIC OCEAN

AUSTRALIA

SOUTH AMERICA

MAP KEY
▲ Major volcano

Write a sentence to answer each question.

1. Human Environment/Interaction How did the 1923 earthquake affect Tokyo?

_____

2. Movement What can happen when there is movement of Earth's plates?

_____

3. Place What kind of place is Mount Fuji?

_____

◆ Vocabulary

Match Up   Finish the sentences in Group A with words from Group B. Write the letter of each correct answer on the blank line.

Group A	Group B
1. One of the main religions of Japan is _____.	**A.** bonsai
2. Japanese robes are called _____.	**B.** terraces
3. A small tree in a flower pot is a _____.	**C.** Shinto
4. Machines that are made to work like people are called _____.	**D.** robots
	E. dormant
5. Large, flat areas of land built into a mountain for growing crops are called _____.	**F.** kimonos
6. When a volcano is not active, it is _____.	

◆ Read and Remember

Finish the Paragraph   Use the words in dark print to finish the paragraph below. Write the words you choose on the correct blank line.

archipelago   **constitutional monarchy**   **pollution**   **raw materials**
forests   **Honshu**   **Tokyo**

Japan is an _____ country with many islands. The largest

island is _____. Most of Japan is covered with mountains and

_____. Japan imports large amounts of _____

for its factories. Japan's government is a _____ because the

emperor has no power. The emperor lives in _____, the country's

capital. One of Japan's biggest problems is _____.

◆ Think and Apply

Drawing Conclusions   Read each pair of sentences. Then look in the box for the conclusion you might make. Write the letter of the conclusion on the blank.

1. Most of Japan is covered with mountains.
There are narrow plains near the coast.

Conclusion: _____

2. Japan has a large fishing industry.
Japan uses the seas for shipping and trading.

Conclusion: _____

3. Japan must import all of its oil and coal.
Japan must import raw materials for industry.

Conclusion: _____

4. The Japanese bow when they say hello and goodbye.
The Japanese remove their shoes before going into a home.

Conclusion: _____

5. Japan exports more goods than it imports.
Japan limits the amount of goods it buys from other countries.

Conclusion: _____

Conclusions
   A. The seas are important to Japan.
   B. Japan does not have much farmland.
   C. Japan has a favorable balance of trade.
   D. Japan has few natural resources.
   E. Traditions are important in Japan.

◆ Journal Writing

Japan is a crowded country with few resources. Write a paragraph in your journal that tells how Japan became a rich industrial country.

Reviewing Bar Graphs

The **bar graph** on this page shows the population of the eight largest cities in Japan. The key shows the islands where the cities are located. Look at all the bars on the graph. Then write the answer to each question.

1. What is the population of Tokyo? _____

2. Which cities are not on Honshu? _____

3. Which two cities have the same population? _____

4. What city has the second largest population? _____

5. Which city has the smallest population? _____

6. How many people live in Osaka? _____

7. How many people live in Fukuoka? _____

8. How many cities have more than 3 million people? _____

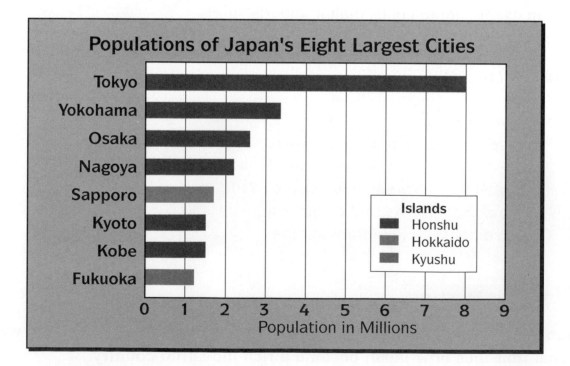

CHAPTER 21

North and South Korea: A Divided Land

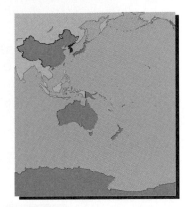

Where Can You Find?
Where can you find a strip of land that separates North and South Korea?

Think About As You Read

1. How did Korea become two countries?
2. How are the two Koreas alike and different?
3. How has South Korea changed since 1953?

New Words

◆ Confucianism
◆ allies
◆ Demilitarized Zone

People and Places

◆ Korean Peninsula
◆ Pyongyang
◆ Seoul

If you lived in South Korea, you would never see your family members who live in North Korea. People in the two countries cannot send letters to each other. They cannot make phone calls to each other. As you read this chapter, find out why Korea is a divided land.

Landforms and Climate of the Korean Peninsula

North and South Korea share the Korean Peninsula. China and Russia are Korea's northern neighbors. The Sea of Japan is between Korea and Japan.

Many parts of the peninsula are covered with forests. Mountains cover most of the Korean Peninsula. So most land cannot be farmed. The east coast is mountainous. Plains cover the western coast and part of the south. Most people live on these plains. Most Korean farmland is on these plains.

Most of Korea has warm summers and cold winters. Korea receives rain throughout the year. But monsoon winds bring heavy rain from June to August.

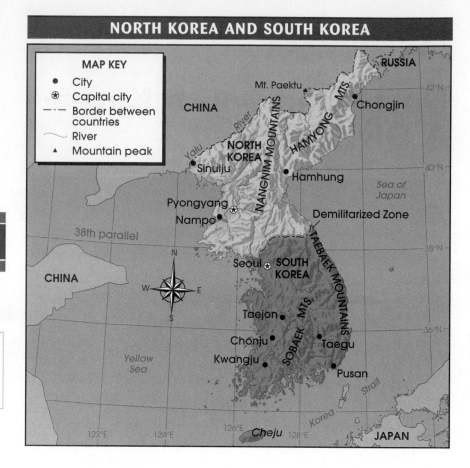

NORTH KOREA AND SOUTH KOREA

MAP KEY
- City
- ⊛ Capital city
- –·–· Border between countries
- ⌇ River
- ▲ Mountain peak

North Korea's Flag

South Korea's Flag

Culture and History

For hundreds of years, all Koreans shared the same culture. The people of North and South Korea speak the Korean language. They write with the Korean alphabet. Education is an important part of Korea's culture. Koreans also have great respect for parents and older people.

Korea's history began long ago. About 4,500 years ago, Koreans started a small country near Pyongyang. Pyongyang is now the capital of North Korea. Later, different Korean tribes ruled different parts of the peninsula. At times China conquered and ruled part of the peninsula. The Chinese brought Buddhism and **Confucianism** to Korea. Confucianism is a way of living based on the teachings of Confucius.

North and South Korea were one country for most of the nation's history. Japan won control of Korea in 1910. It ruled Korea until World War II ended in 1945.

In 1948 Korea was divided at the 38th parallel, or line of latitude. North Korea had a Communist

All Koreans share a very old culture.

government. The Soviet Union and China were its **allies**, or friends. South Korea had a non-Communist government. The United States was South Korea's ally.

In 1950, North Korea invaded South Korea. This was the start of the Korean War. North Korea's goal was to unite the entire country under a Communist government. The United Nations sent soldiers to help South Korea. Most of the soldiers were Americans. China helped North Korea. The war ended in 1953. South Korea remained an independent country.

But North and South Korea continue to be separated. A strip of land that is two and a half miles wide separates the two Koreas at the 38th parallel. This strip of land is called the **Demilitarized Zone**, or DMZ. No one lives on this land. Soldiers are not allowed on this land. Soldiers from both sides guard the borders of their countries at the DMZ. The United States has thousands of soldiers in South Korea. They help guard South Korea's border.

In 1972 and 1991 North and South Korea tried to have peace talks. But the two Koreas are still enemies.

South Korean troops guarding the border at the DMZ

Looking at North Korea

North Korea has 24 million people. More than half of the people live in cities or towns.

North Korea is more mountainous than South Korea. It has many natural resources. It has plenty of coal, copper, iron, and lead.

North Korea is a poor country. Its Communist government owns all of the country's factories and businesses. Factories do not make enough consumer goods. All farmers work on large collective farms. The farmers do not grow enough food. In 1995, 1996, and 1997 there were serious food shortages.

There is no freedom in North Korea. People cannot speak or write against the government. The government controls the newspapers and the radio and television stations.

North Korea is less developed than South Korea. Its factories do not have as much modern technology. It has only one large city. That city, Pyongyang, has more

Pyongyang is the only large city in North Korea.

Seoul, South Korea

than 2 million people. Few people own their own cars in North Korea. Many people in the cities ride bicycles.

Looking at South Korea

South Korea was a poor country when the Korean War ended. Most people were farmers. Since then South Korea has built many factories and industries. It is now a rich industrial country. People enjoy a higher standard of living than people in North Korea.

South Korea has few natural resources. Like Japan, it must import raw materials. South Korea uses imported raw materials to make many products. Today South Korean factories produce clothes, cars, ships, steel, and electronic products. Each year it earns more and more money from exporting its products.

Today South Korea has about 45 million people. South Korea is smaller than North Korea, but its population is larger. So it is more crowded.

This factory in South Korea produces cars for export.

About three fourths of South Koreans live in large cities. Many people move to the cities to get jobs. Some large cities are very crowded. Seoul, the capital, is a modern city with more than 10 million people.

People enjoy life in South Korea. Farmers grow enough food. The middle class is growing. People are earning higher salaries. Many people own cars.

South Koreans are also enjoying more freedom. For years after the Korean War ended, different groups tried to rule the country. Sometimes people could not criticize the government. But in 1987 the country wrote a new constitution. It allows more democracy and freedom.

No one knows what the future of the two Koreas will be. Many Koreans hope that one day their country will be united again.

Chapter Main Ideas

1. North Korea is a poor Communist country. South Korea is a rich non-Communist country.
2. The Korean War began in 1950 when North Korea invaded South Korea. The war ended in 1953.
3. The Demilitarized Zone separates North and South Korea at the 38th parallel.

◆ Vocabulary

Find the Meaning Write the word or words that best complete each sentence. Write your answers on the blank lines.

1. The **Demilitarized Zone** in Korea is a region with _____.

   many soldiers   many cities   no soldiers or weapons

2. **Confucianism** is the way of living based on the _____ of Confucius.

   language   teachings   alphabet

3. During a war, your **allies** will _____.

   be your enemies   attack your cities   help you fight

◆ Read and Remember

Write the Answer Write one or more sentences to answer each question.

1. What kinds of landforms are on the Korean Peninsula? _____

   _____

2. When did Japan rule Korea? _____

   _____

3. How did the Korean War begin? _____

   _____

4. Where is the Demilitarized Zone? _____

   _____

5. What are North Korea's resources? _____

   _____

6. What are two problems in North Korea? _____

   _____

7. How is the economy of South Korea like that of Japan? _____

_____

8. What kinds of products are made in South Korea? _____

_____

9. How did the 1987 constitution help the people of South Korea? _____

_____

◆ Think and Apply

Compare and Contrast   Read each phrase below. Decide whether it tells about North, South Korea, or both. Write the number of the phrase in the correct part of the Venn diagram. If the phrase tells about both nations, write the number in the center of the diagram.

1. a poor developing country

2. many natural resources

3. a rich industrial country

4. people speak the Korean language

5. land has many mountains

6. non-Communist government

7. farmland on the plains

8. Communist government

9. few natural resources

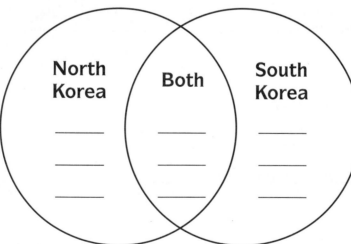

◆ Journal Writing

Write a paragraph in your journal that tells how life has improved in South Korea since 1953. Tell three or more ways the country has become a better place to live.

Reviewing a Physical Map

You learned that a **physical map** helps you find out about the elevation of a region. The physical map on this page shows where there are plains and mountains in Korea. The map shows the elevation of the mountains. Use the map key to know which colors show higher and lower elevations.

Study the map below. Then finish each sentence with an answer in dark print.

6,500–13,000	**Seoul**	**southwest**	**10,000**
9,000	**lower**	**north**	**0–650**

1. There are no mountains in Korea that are more than _____ feet.

2. Land near Mount Paektu has an elevation between _____ feet.

3. Mount Paektu has an elevation of about _____ feet.

4. From this map we can conclude that the elevation of Pyongyang is the same as the city of _____.

5. The elevation in the _____ is less than 650 feet.

6. The elevation of the city of Pusan is _____ than Kanggye.

7. The west coast of Korea has an elevation of _____ feet.

8. We can conclude that there are more mountains in the _____.

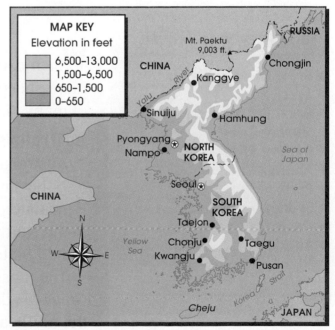

Physical Map of North Korea and South Korea

CHAPTER 22

Australia: A Country and a Continent

Where Can You Find?
Where can you find a huge rock that is more than one mile long?

Think About As You Read

1. What kind of region is Australia's outback?
2. Why did the British first settle in Australia?
3. Why are sheep important in both Australia and New Zealand?

New Words

- outback
- coral reef
- gold rush
- sparsely populated
- artesian wells
- stations
- two-way radios

People and Places

Great Dividing Range
Ayers Rock
Great Barrier Reef
Murray River
Darling River
Aborigines
Perth
Sydney
Canberra
Auckland

Which country is also a continent? Which country has more sheep than people? Which country is the home of many kinds of kangaroos? The answer is Australia.

Australia's Landforms

Australia is the driest and flattest continent. It is also the smallest continent. Australia is in the Southern Hemisphere. The seasons are the opposite of those in the Northern Hemisphere. When it is winter in the United States, it is summer in Australia.

The most important mountains in Australia are the Great Dividing Range. These low mountains begin in the northeast. They continue to the southeast. Fertile coastal plains are to the east and to the south of the mountains. These plains have most of Australia's cities and people. They have the best farmland.

The huge area to the west of the Great Dividing Range is covered with plains, plateaus, and low hills.

AUSTRALIA

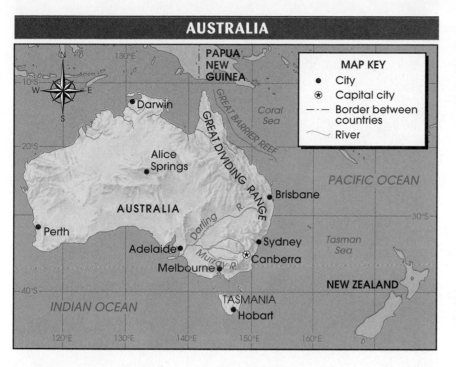

MAP KEY
- City
- ⊛ Capital city
- –·– Border between countries
- ⌒ River

There are few large cities in Australia. What is the name of the only city on the west coast?

Australia's flag

Deserts cover at least one third of the country. The interior of Australia is called the **outback**.

One of the most interesting places in the interior is Ayers Rock. This huge red-brown rock is more than 1,000 feet high. It is more than one mile long.

The Great Barrier Reef is in the ocean near northeastern Australia. It is the world's largest **coral reef**. A coral reef is made from the skeletons of millions of tiny sea animals.

There are few rivers in Australia. The Murray and Darling rivers are the country's only long rivers.

Climate and Resources

Australia has many climates. Northern Australia is in the tropics. The north is always hot. Some places have tropical rain forests. The interior has a hot desert climate. The coastal plains near the Pacific Ocean get enough rain. All of Australia's large cities are on the coastal plains. Southern Australia has a temperate climate.

Australia is rich in natural resources. The country has coal, uranium, and bauxite. It exports more iron than any other nation. It has oil and natural gas. Australia exports minerals to Japan and other Asian countries.

Ayers Rock

The Great Barrier Reef is the largest coral reef in the world.

Koalas

Australia has plants and animals that are not found in any other part of the world. Kangaroos and koalas are two of the animals that come from Australia.

History, Government, and Culture

The first people in Australia were the Aborigines. In 1788 the British started a colony in Australia for some of its prisoners. Later, British people who were not prisoners also settled in Australia. In 1851 gold was discovered. The country had a **gold rush**. People moved to the continent in order to find gold.

Australia became independent from Great Britain in 1901. Since then, it has been a member of the Commonwealth of Nations. Australia is a democracy. It is also a constitutional monarchy. Great Britain's queen, Queen Elizabeth, is also Australia's queen. A prime minister leads the country.

Australia is **sparsely populated**. It is a big country with only 18 million people. About one percent of the people are Aborigines. About four percent are Asian immigrants. Most Australians are white people. Their families once lived in Europe.

Australian culture includes some of the British culture. English is the official language. Like the British, Australians drive their cars on the left side of the road. They celebrate Queen Elizabeth's birthday.

The Aborigines have their own culture. They have their own songs and music. They make beautiful paintings.

Cities and the Outback

Most Australians live in cities. There are five cities with more than one million people. Perth is the only city on the west coast. The largest cities are in the southeast. Sydney is the largest city. This southeastern port has almost 4 million people. Canberra, the capital, is also in this region.

Sydney harbor

The outback has underground water in **artesian wells**. The water in these wells comes to the surface without being pumped. This water is used to raise sheep and cattle.

People in the outback raise sheep and cattle on large ranches called **stations**. Australia has almost ten times more sheep than people. It exports more wool than any other nation.

Life can be lonely on a sheep station in the outback. A station can be hundreds of miles from the closest town. Most outback children live very far from all schools. So they study at home with a program called School of the Air. Special teachers use **two-way radios** to teach outback children who study at home.

The Economy

Australians enjoy a high standard of living. Australia is an industrial nation. It makes many kinds of products. Most of the factory products are used by Australians. They are not sold to other countries. Australia also earns a lot of money from tourism.

Working on a sheep station in the outback

Australia earns most of its money by exporting farm products. It sells wool, meat, and dairy products to many nations. Australia also exports wheat and fruit. Most of Australia's trade was once with Great Britain. Now most trade is with Japan, New Zealand, and the United States.

Many Aborigines have kept their old ways.

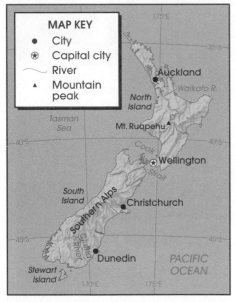

New Zealand

Australia is a flat, dry continent.

New Zealand: Australia's Nearest Neighbor

New Zealand is about 1,000 miles from Australia. The country has two large islands and some small ones. It is sparsely populated. Fewer than 4 million people live in New Zealand.

Like Australia, New Zealand was once a British colony. The British culture is important in New Zealand. Like Australia, the country raises millions of sheep and cattle. Most of its exports are farm products. New Zealand has a high standard of living.

Many parts of New Zealand are covered with mountains. The climate is cooler than Australia's. The country gets plenty of rain. Its largest city, Auckland, has only about 340,000 people.

Looking at Australia's Future

Australia is a large country with lots of dry, empty land. Perhaps one day Australia will find ways to bring water into the dry interior. Until that happens, Australia will be a large country with a small population.

Chapter Main Ideas

1. Australia is the flattest and driest continent. It has a lot of land but only 18 million people.
2. Most of Australia's interior has a desert climate. People raise sheep and cattle in the interior.
3. The Aborigines were the first Australians. Australia was a British colony until 1901.

◆ Vocabulary

Finish the Paragraph   Use the words in dark print to finish the paragraph below. Write the words you choose on the correct blank lines.

sparsely populated   **two-way radios**   **coral reefs**   **artesian wells**
outback   **gold rush**   **stations**

Many people moved to Australia after gold was found. A _____ began in 1851. Australia's interior land that is away from the coast is called the _____. The interior has few people. It is _____. Many people raise sheep on large ranches called _____. These ranches have _____ where water comes to the surface without being pumped. Many children in the interior study at home and talk to the teachers of School of the Air by using _____. Beautiful _____ in the ocean are made from the skeletons of tiny sea animals.

◆ Read and Remember

Where Am I?   Read each sentence. Then look at the words in dark print for the name of the place for each sentence. Write the name of the correct place on the blank after each sentence.

Great Dividing Range   **Auckland**   **Perth**   **New Zealand**
Murray and Darling   **Canberra**   **Sydney**

1. "I am in the capital of Australia." _____

2. "I am in the mountains in eastern Australia." _____

3. "I am at the two longest rivers in Australia." _____

4. "I am in Australia's largest city." _____

5. "I am in the only city on Australia's west coast." _____

6. "I am in New Zealand's largest city." _____

7. "I am in a country that is about 1,000 miles from Australia."

_____

◆ Think and Apply

Finding Relevant Information   Imagine you are telling your friend the reasons why Australia is sparsely populated. Read each sentence below. Decide which sentences are relevant to what you will say. Put a check (✔) in front of the relevant sentences. Find four relevant sentences.

_____ **1.** Many places get very little rain.

_____ **2.** Deserts cover at least one third of Australia.

_____ **3.** Australia is an industrial nation.

_____ **4.** Sydney is a large port.

_____ **5.** Australia has plants and animals not found in any other part of the world.

_____ **6.** Australia has very few rivers.

_____ **7.** Ayers Rock is more than 1,000 feet tall.

_____ **8.** Australia is rich in natural resources.

_____ **9.** Australia has more sheep than people.

_____ **10.** The interior has a hot desert climate.

◆ Journal Writing

Imagine you are going to spend a week in Australia. Would you want to stay in a city or in the outback? Write a paragraph in your journal that tells where you would stay and why. Give three reasons for your choice.

Comparing Climate and Population Maps

We can learn more about Australia by comparing the **population** and **climate maps** on this page. The climate map shows a temperate, or mild, climate in the southeast. By comparing the two maps, we learn that more people live in the southeast where there is a temperate climate. Finish each sentence in Group A with an answer from Group B. Write the letter for the correct answer on the line.

Group A

1. Most of Australia has a ——— climate.

2. Perth and Adelaide have a ——— climate.

3. Australia has ——— cities with a temperate climate.

4. Alice Springs has ——— people per square mile.

5. Some interior desert areas have ———.

6. ——— has a tropical climate.

7. The highest population density is in the temperate and ——— climates.

Group B

A. Darwin

B. 0–2

C. temperate

D. desert

E. no people

F. tropical

G. four

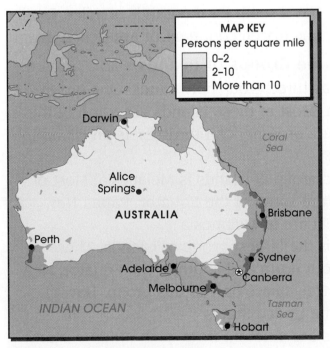

Population Map of Australia

Climate Map of Australia

CHAPTER 23

The Pacific World: Oceania and Antarctica

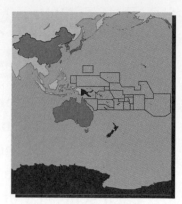

Think About As You Read

1. What are the two kinds of islands in Oceania?
2. How do people earn a living in Oceania?
3. How is Antarctica different from other continents?

New Words

- uninhabited
- atolls
- lagoon
- glaciers
- icebergs
- penguins

People and Places

- Micronesia
- Guam
- Melanesia
- Papua New Guinea
- Fiji
- Polynesia

Imagine going on a long trip through the Pacific Ocean. You will travel through thousands of islands in Oceania. Then you will travel south for thousands of miles. Finally, you will reach the frozen continent of Antarctica.

Oceania: Three Groups of Islands

Oceania has three groups of islands. One group is Micronesia. Most of these islands are north of the Equator. Guam, an American territory, is an island in Micronesia.

The second group of islands is Melanesia. Most of these islands are south of the Equator. Papua New Guinea and Fiji are in Melanesia.

Polynesia is the largest group of islands. These islands are both north and south of the Equator. New Zealand and Hawaii are part of this group. Hawaii is a state in the United States.

The islands are different from each other in many ways. Some islands in Oceania are very small. Other

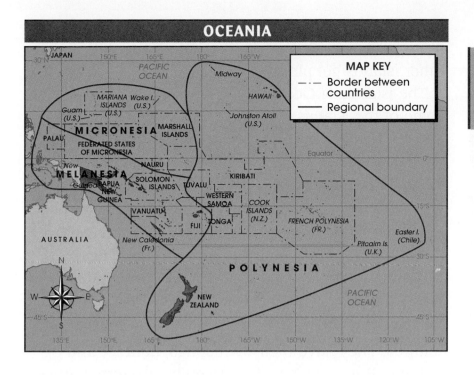

OCEANIA

MAP KEY
- – · – Border between countries
- ——— Regional boundary

JAPAN
PACIFIC OCEAN
Midway
MARIANA ISLANDS (U.S.) Wake I. (U.S.)
Guam (U.S.)
HAWAII
Johnston Atoll (U.S.)
MICRONESIA
MARSHALL ISLANDS
PALAU
FEDERATED STATES OF MICRONESIA
Equator
New Guinea
NAURU
MELANESIA
PAPUA NEW GUINEA
SOLOMON ISLANDS
TUVALU
KIRIBATI
WESTERN SAMOA
VANUATU
COOK ISLANDS (N.Z.)
FIJI TONGA
FRENCH POLYNESIA (FR.)
Easter I. (Chile)
AUSTRALIA
New Caledonia (Fr.)
Pitcairn Is. (U.K.)
POLYNESIA
NEW ZEALAND
PACIFIC OCEAN

islands are very large. New Zealand and New Guinea are the largest islands. The eastern part of New Guinea is called Papua New Guinea. You read in Chapter 16 that the western part of the island belongs to Indonesia.

About 13 million people live on thousands of islands in Oceania. Some islands have more than a million people. But most islands have fewer than 500,000 people. Many islands are **uninhabited**, or without people.

The Islands, Their Climates, and Their Resources

Oceania has two kinds of islands. There are high islands and low islands. High islands are made of mountains and volcanoes. Most high islands have fertile soil. Forests and jungles cover many high islands. Earthquakes and typhoons often cause great damage. Hawaii, New Zealand, and Guam are high islands.

Most of the low islands are called **atolls**. They are made of coral reefs. Often the coral reef surrounds a body of water. That water is called a **lagoon**. Atolls do not have fertile soil for farming. People who live on these islands get most of their food from the sea. Huge waves called tsunamis often cause great damage to the low islands.

Coral reef and atoll

Pineapples growing on a plantation in Hawaii

Most Pacific islands are in the tropics. So they have a warm climate. Some islands receive very little rain. Other islands get plenty of rain for farming.

The islands of Oceania have few natural resources. Some of the islands get timber from their forests. New Guinea is one of the few islands that has some minerals. It has silver, gold, copper, and some oil.

Culture and Education

The people of Oceania speak about 1,200 different languages. English is spoken more than any other language.

Most people in Oceania are Christians. Some people follow traditional island religions.

The people of Oceania enjoy their own traditional cultures. They have their own songs, dances, and clothing. But many people also enjoy western culture.

Most islands have elementary schools for their children. Some have high schools. Guam and Fiji are two of the islands that have universities. Thousands of students from other islands go to the university in Fiji.

Standard of Living and Earning a Living

The people of Hawaii and New Zealand enjoy high standards of living. These islands are the only developed areas in Oceania. Other islands have a low standard of living. On these developing islands, most people live in small villages.

There are very few ways to earn a living in most parts of Oceania. On the low islands, many people work at fishing. On the high islands, people work at both fishing and farming. They export such cash crops as sugarcane, pineapples, coffee, and coconuts.

Tourists enjoy the beach of Fiji.

Many people earn a living in Oceania through tourism. Thousands of people visit the beaches of Fiji, Guam, and other islands. Many islands could earn more money by developing their tourist industries.

Antarctica: The Coldest Continent

Antarctica is the continent at the South Pole. No one has a permanent home on this continent. A few thousand scientists work in Antarctica. They do research to learn about Earth.

Glaciers cover the tall mountains of Antarctica.

Antarctica is covered with thick ice. It has many tall mountains. Thick sheets of slow-moving ice called **glaciers** cover these mountains. There are also huge mountains of ice called **icebergs** in the nearby oceans.

Antarctica is really a frozen desert. In summer the temperature stays close to 32°F. In winter it can get as cold as 100°F below zero. The continent gets very little rain or snow.

Seals, whales, and **penguins** enjoy the icy ocean near Antarctica. Penguins are birds that cannot fly. They live on the land and swim in icy waters.

Antarctica has many minerals. But it is too difficult to mine minerals in this frozen land.

Oceania and Antarctica have few of the world's resources or factories. But they are important because they cover a large area of Earth.

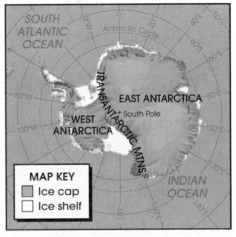

Antarctica

Chapter Main Ideas

1. Micronesia, Melanesia, and Polynesia are three groups of islands in the Pacific.
2. Oceania has low islands made of coral reefs. It has high islands made of mountains and volcanoes.
3. Antarctica is a mountainous continent that is covered with thick ice.

Penguins

◆ Vocabulary

Finish Up   Choose the word in dark print that best completes each sentence. Write the word on the correct blank line.

atolls   uninhabited   glaciers   lagoon   penguins   icebergs

1. Huge mountains of ice in the ocean are _____.

2. Low islands that are made of coral reefs are _____.

3. Many coral reefs surround a body of water called a _____.

4. A place that has no people is _____.

5. Birds that live in Antarctica and swim in its oceans are _____.

6. Huge slow-moving sheets of ice are _____.

◆ Read and Remember

Matching   Each item in Group B tells about an item in Group A. Write the letter of each item in Group B next to the correct answer in Group A.

Group A

_____ **1.** Micronesia

_____ **2.** Polynesia

_____ **3.** scientists

_____ **4.** Fiji and Guam

_____ **5.** high islands

_____ **6.** Hawaii

_____ **7.** atoll

Group B

A. These islands are made of mountains and volcanoes.

B. These workers do research in Antarctica.

C. This group of islands is north of the Equator.

D. This type of island does not have fertile soil.

E. This is the largest island group in Oceania.

F. These islands have universities.

G. These Pacific Islands are a state in the United States.

Write the Answer   Write one or more sentences to answer each question.

1. What island in Micronesia is an American Territory? _____

_____

2. About how many people live in Oceania? _____

_____

3. How do people on high islands earn a living? _____

_____

4. Why is Antarctica a desert? _____

_____

◆ Think and Apply

Fact or Opinion   Write **F** next to each fact below. Write **O** next to each opinion. You should find five sentences that are opinions.

_____ **1.** New Guinea and New Zealand are the largest islands in Oceania.

_____ **2.** High islands have more fertile soil than low islands.

_____ **3.** More people should settle on atolls.

_____ **4.** Guam is a better place for tourists than Fiji.

_____ **5.** Polynesia is the largest group of islands.

_____ **6.** New Zealand and Hawaii are the most developed islands in Oceania.

_____ **7.** The people of Papua New Guinea should work harder to mine their minerals.

_____ **8.** Tourism is the best way for the Pacific islands to earn money.

_____ **9.** People should start mining Antarctica's minerals.

_____ **10.** There are no cities or villages in Antarctica.

◆ Journal Writing

Write a paragraph in your journal that tells why it is difficult to earn a living on most Pacific islands. Give at least two reasons.

CHAPTER 24

The Future of East Asia and the Pacific

Where Can You Find?
Where can you find a country whose people are working hard to protect the environment by recycling?

Think About As You Read

1. Where is overcrowding a problem in East Asia?
2. Why is a lack of democracy a problem in China and North Korea?
3. What are some nations doing to protect the environment?

New Words

◆ population growth rate
◆ human rights
◆ environment
◆ enforced

People and Places

◆ Tibet

Many countries in East Asia and the Pacific have strong economies. Some countries like Japan and Australia have very high standards of living. In some places people struggle to get enough food. This region must solve four problems so that all of its people can have a better life.

Overcrowded Nations

China, Japan, Hong Kong, Taiwan, and South Korea are all overcrowded. They do not have enough farmland. So it is difficult for some of the East Asian countries to feed their people. In Hong Kong and the cities of Japan most people live in small homes and apartments. In some cities in China, two families must sometimes share a tiny apartment.

East Asian countries are looking for ways to solve this problem. In Japan most people try to have small families. You learned that China's laws allow couples

A crowded apartment building in Shanghai, China

to have only one or two children. China's population is now growing more slowly. Its **population growth rate** has dropped to about one percent a year. But more than 15 million Chinese children are born each year. It will be very hard for China to feed such a large population.

A Lack of Democracy

China and North Korea are countries with dictators and Communist governments. Today China and North Korea do not allow **human rights**. Human rights are the rights that give people freedom and safety. People in China and North Korea cannot practice religion. They cannot speak or write against the government. In 1951 China took control of its southern neighbor, Tibet. It is now difficult for people in Tibet to practice their Buddhist religion. Now that Hong Kong is part of China, its people have less freedom to protest against the government.

China now trades with the United States, Japan, and other democratic nations. Perhaps these trading partners will pressure China to allow more freedom.

Communism ended in Eastern Europe and Russia in the early 1990s. Many people hope that communism will one day end in China and North Korea, too.

The Chinese have destroyed many Buddhist shrines in Tibet.

The Need to Protect the Environment

The nations of East Asia and the Pacific must find ways to protect their **environment**. The environment is the land, air, and water of a region.

Pollution has become a very big problem in China. China burns coal in order to make most of its energy. The country has air pollution from burning lots of coal. China also has acid rain. Pollution mixes with the rain and becomes acid rain. China's acid rain has damaged its forests, lakes, and rivers. Cities and villages in China also have water pollution problems. Much of the water in China is not safe to drink. China has passed laws to stop pollution. But it has not **enforced**, or carried out, these laws.

Japan also has pollution problems because it has so many cars and factories. Sometimes city air is so polluted that people wear special masks when they go outside. Japan has passed and enforced laws to protect the environment. Now the air and water are much less polluted.

The Japanese are also protecting their environment by recycling. They work hard to recycle as much as possible. They recycle paper, glass, plastics, and many other materials. They make new products from their old products. Recycling is helping Japan save important resources for the future.

Cars and factories cause pollution in the Pacific, too. Australia's big cities have pollution problems. Some of the cities on the Pacific islands are also starting to have pollution problems. In the years ahead, these countries must find ways to keep their air and water clean.

Keeping Old Traditions in Modern Nations

Traditions have always been important in East Asia. For hundreds of years, the teachings of Confucius guided the people of China and Korea. Many of these traditions have been lost under communism. People throughout Oceania have enjoyed different kinds of traditions. Can countries keep their traditions and still be modern nations? Japan has proved that it is possible.

Burning coal causes very bad air pollution in China.

The Japanese have been able to keep their ancient traditions and still be a modern nation.

These cans in Japan will be recycled to make new products.

Working for the Future

Most people in East Asia and the Pacific have a better life than their parents had. They have more food and better technology. They have better schools and industries.

You have read about many different countries and cultures. There are a lot of changes taking place in the world today. The Green Revolution is helping farmers in India grow enough food to feed its people. South Korea is becoming a more democratic country. Apartheid ended in South Africa in 1994.

Every day people in all parts of the world try to solve different kinds of problems. You have read about these problems in this book. Illiteracy, hunger, war, pollution, and a lack of freedom are some of the biggest problems. People in every country are working to have a better future. Perhaps you, too, will work for a better tomorrow for our world.

A good education for this school girl in Fiji will give her a better future.

Chapter Main Ideas

1. Most countries in East Asia are overcrowded. It is difficult to feed their huge populations.
2. Millions of people in China and North Korea do not enjoy human rights.
3. As nations have more cars and factories, they have more pollution problems.

◆ Vocabulary

Match Up Finish the sentences in Group A with words from Group B. Write the letter of each correct answer on the blank line.

Group A

1. The _____ tells you how much a population grows and changes during a year.

2. The rights that protect the freedom and safety of

people are called _____.

3. The land, air, and water of a region are the _____.

4. A law is _____ when it is carried out.

Group B

A. human rights

B. population growth rate

C. enforced

D. environment

◆ Read and Remember

Complete the Chart Use the facts from the chapter to complete the chart. You can read the chapter again to find facts you do not remember.

Problems of East Asia and the Pacific

	What Is the Problem?	How Does the Problem Hurt the Region?	What Is One Way the Problem Is Being Solved?
1.			
2.			
3.			

Find the Main Idea   Read the five sentences below. Choose the main idea and write it in the main idea box. Then find three sentences that support the main idea. Write them in the boxes of the main idea chart. There will be one sentence in the group that you will not use.

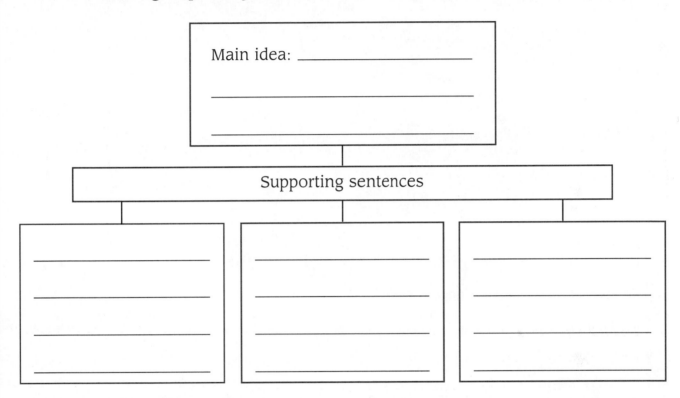

Main idea: _____

_____

_____

Supporting sentences

a. The Chinese government does not allow Buddhists in Tibet to practice their religion.

b. China has serious pollution problems.

c. China does not allow people to speak or write against the government.

d. China does not allow democracy and human rights.

e. The Chinese government stopped the student protests at Tiananmen Square.

◆ **Journal Writing**

Write a paragraph about one problem in East Asia and the Pacific. Then tell two or three ways nations may solve that problem.

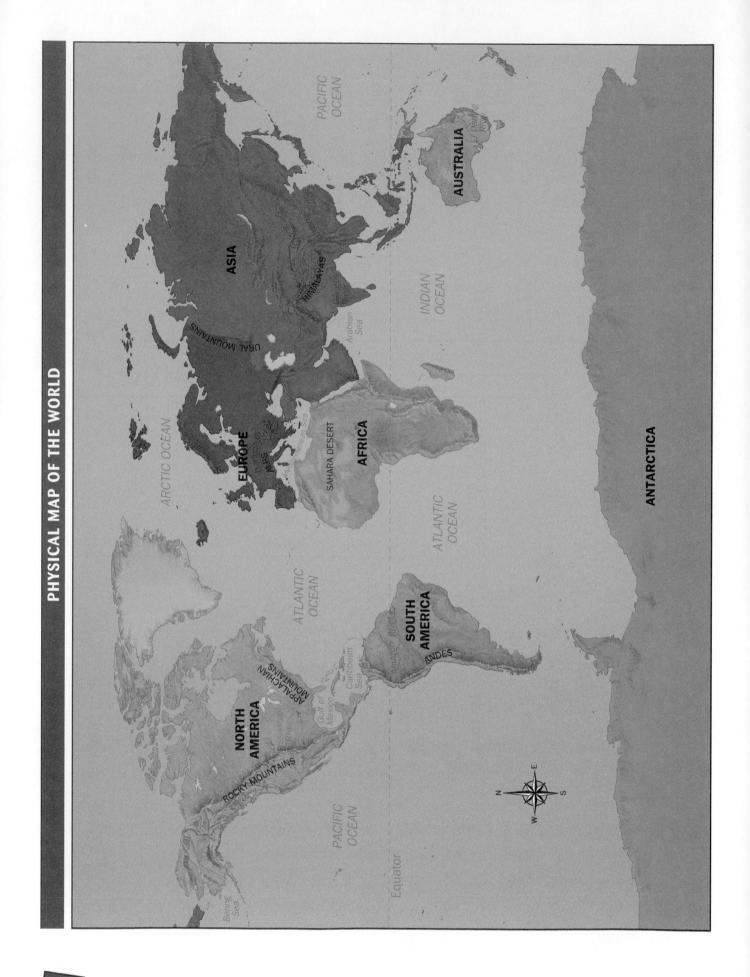

GLOSSARY

aba (page 86)   An aba is a long black robe that covers a Muslim woman's head, face, and body.

absolute monarchy (page 85)   In an absolute monarchy, the king or queen has full power to make all laws.

acupuncture (page 149)   Acupuncture is a system that uses small needles put into different parts of the body to treat disease and pain.

AIDS (page 44)   AIDS is a serious disease that has no cure.

ally (page 165)   An ally is a country that joins another country in a common cause.

ancient (page 61)   Ancient means very old.

apartheid (page 35)   Apartheid laws in South Africa kept racial groups apart. Apartheid ended in 1991.

aquifer (page 92)   An aquifer is an area of underground water.

archipelago (page 122)   An archipelago is a chain of islands.

artesian well (page 173)   Water in an artesian well comes to the surface without being pumped.

assemble (page 13)   To assemble means to put parts together.

atoll (page 179)   An atoll is a low island made of coral reefs.

average (page 117)   Average means usual.

Bahasa Indonesia (page 125)   Bahasa Indonesia is the official language of Indonesia.

billionaire (page 29)   A billionaire is a person who has more than one billion (one thousand million) dollars.

boat people (page 117)   Boat people were non-Communist refugees who escaped from Vietnam in small boats at the end of the Vietnam War.

bonsai (page 156)   A bonsai is a tiny tree grown in a pot, usually in Japanese gardens.

Buddhism (page 100)   Buddhism is a religion based on the teachings of Buddha.

cape (page 33)   A cape is a point of land that sticks out into a large body of water.

cassava (page 12)   A cassava is an African vegetable.

caste (page 107)   A caste is a group of people in the Hindu religion.

caste system (page 107)   The caste system is the way people in India are divided into groups.

cemetery (page 91)   A cemetery is a place where people are buried.

character (page 149)   A character is a little picture that stands for a word or an idea in Japanese, Chinese, and other languages.

chemical fertilizer (page 60)   A chemical fertilizer is a mixture of chemicals added to soil to make plants grow better.

Christianity (page 53)   Christianity is the Christian religion.

chromite (page 77)   Chromite is a mineral used to make chrome, a shiny metal that does not rust.

collective (page 147)   A collective is a huge government-owned farm in China.

colored (page 35)   A colored person in South Africa has black and white or black and Asian parents.

commercial agriculture (page 102) Commercial agriculture is a type of farming in which cash crops are grown on large plantations.

communicate (page 125) To communicate means to give information.

Communist party (page 117) The Communist party is the government of a Communist country.

conflict (page 29)   A conflict is a fight that often lasts a long time.

Confucianism (page 164)   Confucianism is a way of living based on the teachings of Confucius.

conservation (page 92)   Conservation means to save natural resources.

contract (page 147)   A contract is a legal agreement between two groups that tells what each group can do.

coral reef (page 171)   A coral reef is made from the skeletons of millions of tiny sea animals.

crossroads (page 50)   A crossroads is the place where roads meet.

delta (page 11)   A delta is land made of soil that a river has carried and left at the place where the river flows into the sea.

Demilitarized Zone (page 165) The DMZ is a strip of land that separates North Korea from South Korea at the 38th parallel.

demonstration (page 146) A demonstration is a public meeting where groups of people show how they feel.

deposited (page 59)   Soil is deposited by a river when it is left behind.

desalination plant (page 87) A desalination plant takes the salt out of ocean water to make fresh water.

desertification (page 42) Desertification occurs when deserts grow larger and grasslands become smaller.

dike (page 148)   A dike is a special wall built to control floods.

disease (page 44)   Disease means sickness.

dormant (page 159)   Dormant means quiet. A dormant volcano may erupt again.

drip irrigation (page 67)   Drip irrigation conserves water by using hoses to water individual plants.

drought (page 4)   A drought is a long period of time without rain.

enforced (page 186)   Enforced means carried out.

environment (page 186) The environment is the land, air, and water of a region.

erosion (page 43)   Erosion takes place when soil is blown away by wind or washed away by rain.

escarpment (page 34)   An escarpment is a steep cliff.

expert (page 44)   An expert is a person with special skills or knowledge.

extended family (page 107)   In an extended family, relatives such as grandparents, aunts, uncles, cousins, children, and parents all live together.

famine (page 42)   A famine is a terrible shortage of food for a long period of time.

ferry boat (page 123)   A ferry boat carries people across small bodies of water.

foreign (page 85)   People are foreign if they come from another country.

foreign aid (page 44)   Foreign aid is money and help that one nation gives to another nation.

foreign investment (page 132) A foreign investment is made when business owners use their money to start businesses in other countries.

free enterprise (page 141)   Free enterprise means people can own and control their own businesses.

glacier (page 181)   A glacier is a thick sheet of slow-moving ice that covers the mountains of Antarctica.

gold rush (page 172)   In a gold rush, people move to an area where gold has been discovered.

gorge (page 46)   A gorge is a deep valley with steep rocky walls.

grassland (page 4)   A grassland is an area covered with grass.

Green Revolution (page 132) The Green Revolution means farmers in developing countries use miracle seeds and modern farming methods to grow large crops.

Hajj (page 86)   A Hajj is the visit to Mecca that all Muslims must make at least once.

Hebrew (page 53)   Hebrew is the official language of Israel.

herb (page 149)   An herb is a plant whose parts are used to make medicines.

Hindi (page 106)   Hindi is the main official language of India.

Hinduism (page 100)   Hinduism is the main religion of India.

homeland (page 69)   A homeland is a person's native country.

human rights (page 185)   Human rights are the rights that give people freedom and safety.

humid (page 124)   A humid climate is damp.

hunger (page 41)   Hunger means there is not enough food.

iceberg (page 181)   An iceberg is a huge mountain of ice in the ocean.

inland (page 140)   An inland area is far from the ocean.

investing (page 118)   Investing is when business owners use their money to start other businesses and develop an area.

Islamic fundamentalism (page 58) Under Islamic fundamentalism, Muslims follow the strictest rules of Islam.

Judaism (page 52)   Judaism is the religion of the Jews.

jute (page 109)   Jute is used to make rope.

Kaaba (page 86)   The Kaaba is the holiest place in Islam. It is located in the Great Mosque at Mecca.

kibbutz (page 68)   A kibbutz is a farm in Israel owned by its members who share all of the work.

kimono (page 156)   A kimono is a traditional Japanese robe.

Koran (page 53)   The Koran is the holy book of Muslims. Muhammad's teachings are in the Koran.

lagoon (page 179)   A lagoon is a body of water surrounded by a coral reef.

Lingala (page 28)   Lingala is an African language spoken in Congo.

loan (page 44)   A loan is money that one nation lends another.

mainland (page 139)   A mainland is the main area of a region, not including the islands off its coast.

malnutrition (page 29)   Malnutrition is poor health caused by lack of good food.

manganese (page 62)   Manganese is a metal ore.

manufacturing (page 117) Manufacturing means making products in a factory.

minority (page 35)   A minority is a small part of the population.

miracle seeds (page 132)   Miracle seeds are special seeds that produce larger crops.

missile (page 93)   A missile is a weapon with bombs.

modest (page 86)   To be modest means to be proper.

monotheism (page 52)   Monotheism is the belief in one God.

monsoon (page 98)   A monsoon is a seasonal wind.

national park (page 21) A national park is a government-owned area where wild animals are protected.

natural disaster (page 140) A natural disaster is a terrible event caused by nature. Volcanoes, earthquakes, typhoons, and tsunamis are all natural disasters.

nomad (page 19) A nomad moves from place to place looking for food and water for his animals.

oasis (page 52) An oasis is a place in the desert that has underground water.

oil refinery (page 21) In an oil refinery, oil is cleaned and changed into products such as gasoline.

okapi (page 27) The okapi is a furry animal that lives only in Congo's rain forests. It is the symbol of Congo.

OPEC (page 86) OPEC, the Organization of Petroleum Exporting Countries, is an organization of countries that export oil.

orphan (page 110) An orphan is a child whose parents are dead.

orphanage (page 110) An orphanage is a group home for orphans.

Ottoman Empire (page 76) The Ottoman Empire was the area of the Middle East and North Africa controlled by the Ottoman Turks from the 1500s until after World War I.

outback (page 171) The outback is the interior of Australia.

overcrowded (page 14) A place is overcrowded when it has too many people.

overgraze (page 43) Overgrazing is when sheep and cattle destroy an area by eating all the grasses.

overpopulation (page 91) Overpopulation means there are too many people living in a region.

Palestinian Liberation Organization (PLO) (page 70) The PLO is an organization that wants a homeland for the Palestinians in Israel.

parallel (page 116) A parallel is a line of latitude.

Peace Corps (page 45) The Peace Corps is an American group that sends its members to help developing countries.

penguin (page 181) A penguin is a bird that cannot fly. Many penguins enjoy the icy ocean near Antarctica.

pharaoh (page 61) The pharaohs were the kings of ancient Egypt.

phosphate (page 54) Phosphate is a natural resource used to make fertilizers.

population growth rate (page 185) The population growth rate is the number of children born each year as a percent of the total population.

profit (page 147) Profit is the money made after subtracting expenses.

protest (page 146)   To protest is to complain strongly against something.

pyramid (page 61)   The pyramids are large stone structures built in ancient Egypt.

racial group (page 35)   A racial group is a group of people who share physical characteristics such as skin color.

rebel (page 30)   To rebel means to fight against the government.

reelected (page 125)   To be reelected means to be voted into office again.

refugee (page 29)   A refugee is a person who leaves home during a war.

religious order (page 110)   A religious order is a group of people who live and work together under the rules of their religion.

reservoir (page 11)   A reservoir is a place where water is stored for future use.

robot (page 157)   A robot is a machine that looks like a person and can do some of the jobs people do.

sacred (page 105)   Sacred means holy.

Sahel (page 4)   The Sahel is a region of dry grasslands south of the Sahara. The Sahel stretches from the Atlantic Ocean to the Red Sea.

sand dune (page 83)   A sand dune is a hill of sand formed by the wind.

sanitation (page 131)   Sanitation means keeping something like a city clean.

savanna (page 4)   A savanna is a land area with long, thick grass and short trees.

scarce (page 67)   Scarce means hard to get.

secular (page 76)   Secular means not religious.

semiarid (page 4)   A semiarid climate is hot, with rainy and dry seasons.

shah (page 93)   Shah was the title of the king of Iran.

shifting agriculture (page 101)   Shifting agriculture is a type of farming in which people move from place to place chopping down trees and planting crops until the land is no longer fertile.

Shinto (page 156)   Shinto is a religion practiced in Japan. People who believe in the Shinto religion pray to gods found in rivers, mountains, trees, and other forms of nature.

shish kebab (page 77)   Shish kebab is a popular Turkish dish of meat and vegetables cooked on a stick.

Sikhism (page 107)   Sikhism is an Indian religion.

silt (page 59)   Silt is the tiny pieces of soil left behind by a river.

sisal (page 20)   Sisal is a plant used to make rope.

software (page 68)   Software is the information and programs used by a computer.

sparsely populated (page 172) A sparsely populated area has very few people living there.

station (page 173) A station is a large sheep or cattle ranch in Australia.

steppe climate (page 52) A steppe climate gets just enough rain for grasses to grow.

stilt (page 125) A stilt is a pole used to support a house built up off the ground.

strait (page 75) A strait is a narrow body of water that connects two larger bodies of water.

subcontinent (page 100) A subcontinent is a large area of land that is smaller than a continent.

Swahili (page 20) Swahili is the official language of Kenya.

swamp (page 10) A swamp is soft, wet land.

temperate zone (page 140) The temperate zones are the climates north and south of the tropics. The weather in a temperate zone is not too hot or too cold.

terrace (page 157) A terrace is a large, flat area of land built into the side of a hill for planting crops.

Tet Festival (page 116) The Tet Festival is the celebration of the Vietnamese New Year.

textile (page 117) A textile is a kind of cloth.

timber (page 99) Timber is wood used to make buildings and furniture.

traditional method (page 6) A traditional method is the old way of doing things.

tribe (page 5) A tribe is a group of people who share a language, religion, and culture.

tsetse fly (page 44) A tsetse fly is an African insect that causes "sleeping sickness."

tsunami (page 141) A tsunami is a huge, dangerous wave caused by an underwater earthquake.

two-way radio (page 173) A two-way radio allows people to talk to each other.

typhoon (page 115) A typhoon is a dangerous tropical Asian storm.

unfavorable balance of trade (page 62) An unfavorable balance of trade means a country buys more goods from other countries than it exports.

uninhabited (page 179) Uninhabited means without people.

United Nations (page 44) The UN is an organization of countries that work together.

untouchable (page 107) An untouchable is a person who belongs to the lowest group of people in the caste system of India.

urbanization (page 13) Urbanization is the movement of people to cities.

vegetarian (page 107)   A vegetarian is a person who does not eat meat.

vegetation (page 3)   Vegetation is the plants that grow in a region.

Viet Cong (page 116)   During the Vietnam War, the Viet Cong were Communists who lived in South Vietnam.

volcanic ash (page 123)   Volcanic ash is the small pieces of rocks that come out of an erupting volcano.

wet rice farming (page 102)   Wet rice farming is a type of farming in which rice seeds are planted in small flooded fields after heavy rains.

wildlife (page 21)   Wildlife is all the wild animals that live in an area.

yam (page 12)   A yam is a vegetable similar to a sweet potato.

INDEX

Mecca, Saudia Arabia, 84, 86, 87

Medina, Saudia Arabia, 84

Mediterranean climate, 4, 52, 75

Mediterranean Sea, 2, 51, 52, 57, 59, 60, 61, 62, 66, 75

Mekong River, 101, 114, 115, 118

Mekong River delta, 114, 115

Melanesia, 178, 181

Micronesia, 178, 181

Middle East, 5, 6, 49–96, 101

Mobutu, Joseph, 29, 30

Mombasa, Kenya, 18, 20, 22

monsoons, 98–99, 101, 102, 106, 114, 140, 148, 163

Morocco, 57

Mother Teresa, 110

Muhammad, 53, 84

Murray River, 171

Muslims, 5, 14, 20, 49, 53, 58, 66, 71, 76, 77, 79, 84, 85, 86, 87, 93, 100, 107, 108, 125, 126

Nairobi, Kenya, 20

Nasser, Lake, 60

NATO, 79

Negev Desert, 66, 67, 68

New Delhi, India, 109

New Guinea, 122, 179, 180

New Zealand, 137, 138, 140, 141, 142, 159, 173, 174, 178, 179, 180

Niger River, 3, 11

Nigeria, 10–14

Nile Delta, 59, 60

Nile River, 3, 5, 52, 57, 58, 59–60, 61, 62, 93

Nile Valley, 59, 60, 61

Noor, Queen, 94

North Africa, 2, 4, 5, 6, 49, 51, 57, 58, 62

North Korea, 139, 140, 141, 142, 163–166, 185, 186, 187

Northern Hemisphere, 34, 170

oasis, 52, 84

Oceania, 138, 140, 178–180, 181, 186

oil, 5, 10, 11, 12, 14, 21, 26, 28, 36, 49, 53, 54, 62, 77, 83, 86–87, 91, 92, 94, 99, 106, 115, 123, 124, 125–126, 171, 180

Orange River, 34

Organization of Petroleum Exporting Countries (OPEC), 86, 87, 125, 126

outback, 171, 173

Pacific (region), 137–142, 159, 170–187

Pacific Ocean, 98, 126, 137, 138, 155, 159, 171, 178

Pakistan, 100, 101, 108, 132

Palestinian Liberation Organization (PLO), 70, 93

Palestinians, 69, 70, 93

Papua New Guinea, 122, 178, 179

Peace Corps, 45

Persian Gulf, 51, 83, 86, 93

Persian Gulf War, 93

Perth, Australia, 173

Philippines, 100, 101

pollution, 131, 158, 186, 187

Polynesia, 178, 181

Pyongyang, North Korea, 164, 165–166

rain forest, 3, 4, 18, 27, 99, 101, 124, 171

Red River, 114, 115, 118

Red River delta, 114, 115

Red Sea, 2, 4, 51, 59, 83, 84

Ring of Fire, 159

Riyadh, Saudi Arabia, 52, 84, 85

Rwanda, 29, 30

Sahara, 1, 2, 3, 4, 5, 6, 10, 42, 51, 57, 92

Sahel, 4, 11, 42

Sapporo, Japan, 158

Saudi Arabia, 51, 52, 53, 83–87, 91–92, 93

savannas, 4, 10, 19, 27

Seoul, South Korea, 166

Shanghai, China, 149, 185

Shinto, 156